M000167106

Praise for

POLITICAL POLLING IN THE DIGITAL AGE

"I generally have harbored a jaundiced view that nine out of ten polls prove what they set out to prove. This tome challenges these stereotypes. Charlie Cook, in but one example, makes a compelling case that people like me need to immerse ourselves more deeply into the process to separate the kernels of wheat from survey chaff. Later, Mark Blumenthal points out that while it's a jungle out there in present-day Pollsterville, where traditional 'safeguards' are not always the norm, there remains accuracy amid the chaos. Most fascinating is his proposed blueprint to standardize credibility. *Political Polling in the Digital Age* is a long-needed guide in this Age of Polling."

—JAMES E. SHELLEDY, former editor of *The Salt Lake Tribune*

The 2008 presidential election provided a "perfect storm" for pollsters. A significant portion of the population had exchanged their landlines for cellphones, which made them harder to survey. Additionally, a potential Bradley effect—in which white voters misrepresent their intentions of voting for or against a black candidate—skewed predictions, and aggressive voter registration and mobilization campaigns by Barack Obama combined to challenge conventional understandings about how to measure and report public preferences. In the wake of these significant changes, *Political Polling in the Digital Age,* edited by Kirby Goidel, offers timely and insightful interpretations of the impact these trends will have on polling.

In this groundbreaking collection, contributors place recent developments in public-opinion polling into a broader historical context, examine how to construct accurate meanings from public-opinion surveys, and analyze the future of public-opinion polling. Notable contributors include Mark Blumenthal, editor and publisher of Pollster.com; Anna Greenberg, a leading Democratic pollster; and Scott Keeter, director of survey research for the Pew Research Center.

In an era of increasingly personalized and interactive communications, accurate political polling is more difficult and also more important. *Political Polling in the Digital Age* presents fresh perspectives and relevant tactics that demystify the variable world of opinion taking.

Kirby Goidel is director of Louisiana State University's Manship School Research Facility, which includes the Public Policy Research Lab and the Media Effects Lab. As senior public policy fellow of the Reilly Center for Media & Public Affairs, he directs the annual Louisiana Survey and provides analysis of the findings to government organizations and the media. The author of two books and numerous journal articles, he is a professor in the Manship School of Mass Communication and the Department of Political Science.

Charlie Cook is publisher of *The Cook Political Report,* a weekly columnist for *National Journal* and CongressDailyAM, and a political analyst for NBC News.

POLITICAL POLLING IN THE DIGITAL AGE

MEDIA & PUBLIC AFFAIRS
Robert Mann, *Series Editor*

Media & Public Affairs, a book series published by Louisiana State University Press and the Reilly Center for Media & Public Affairs at the Manship School of Mass Communication, LSU, explores the complex relationship between knowledge and power in our democracy. Books in this series examine what citizens and public officials know, where they get their information, and how they use that information to act. For more information, visit www.lsu.edu/mpabookseries.

POLITICAL POLLING IN THE DIGITAL AGE

The Challenge of Measuring and Understanding Public Opinion

Edited by KIRBY GOIDEL

Introduction by CHARLIE COOK

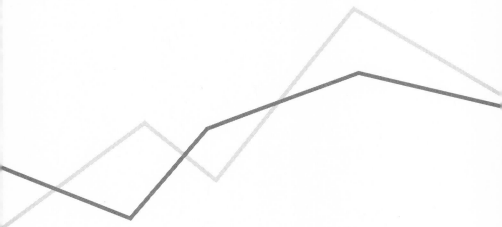

LOUISIANA STATE UNIVERSITY PRESS

BATON ROUGE

Publication of this book is supported by DeeDee and Kevin P. Reilly, Sr.

Published by Louisiana State University Press
Manufactured in the United States of America
LSU Press Paperback Original
First printing

DESIGNER: Amanda McDonald Scallan
TYPEFACES: text, Minion Pro; News Gothic MT, display
PRINTER: McNaughton & Gunn, Inc.
BINDER: Dekker Bookbinding

Library of Congress Cataloging-in-Publication Data

Political polling in the digital age : the challenge of measuring and understanding public opinion / edited by Kirby Goidel; introduction by Charlie Cook.
    p. cm. — (Media & public affairs)
Includes bibliographical references and index.
ISBN 978-0-8071-3829-8 (cloth : alk. paper) — ISBN 978-0-8071-3783-3 (pbk. : alk. paper)
1. Public opinion polls—United States. 2. Digital media—Political aspects—United States. 3. Mass media and public opinion—United States. I. Goidel, Robert K., 1967–
HN90.P8P643 2011
303.3'80973—dc22

2010043002

The paper in this book meets the guidelines for permanence and durability of the Committee on Production Guidelines for Book Longevity of the Council on Library Resources.♾

CONTENTS

ACKNOWLEDGMENTS

The essays in this volume were first presented at the Breaux Symposium held on the LSU campus in October 2009. Each year, the Breaux Symposium brings together leading scholars, journalists, and political professionals to discuss an issue of national importance. I was given the opportunity to organize the 2009 symposium on the topic "The Meaning and Measurement of Public Opinion." Since I am heavily involved in the day-to-day work of survey research, organizing the symposium afforded me the chance to consider more deeply the work that we do in constructing questionnaires and collecting and analyzing survey data.

My first debt of gratitude for this opportunity extends to John Maxwell Hamilton, dean of LSU's Manship School of Mass Communication, and Adrienne Moore, the director of the Reilly Center for Media & Public Affairs. Without their commitment to the project, neither the book nor the symposium would have been possible.

I owe a different debt to the late Tim Cook. Tim was an amazing scholar and a wonderful colleague. His presence, intellectual leadership, rigorous scholarship, and good humor have been deeply missed. The quality of his work in organizing the 2003 Breaux Symposium (published as *Freeing the Presses: The First Amendment in Action* by LSU Press in 2005) served as the standard of excellence to which I aspired in putting this book together.

I also owe a debt to each of our participants—Charlie Cook, Susan Herbst, Mark Blumenthal, Scott Keeter, Anna Greenberg, and Charles Franklin—for taking time out of their busy schedules, traveling to Baton Rouge, and spending an afternoon discussing the future of polling. Listening in on their conversation was an incredibly rewarding experience that can be only partially captured on the printed page.

This project would have been unthinkable without the incredible work of Adrienne Moore and Heather Herman at the Reilly Center for Media & Public Affairs. Adrienne pushed the project forward, offered insightful ideas on the content and organization of the book and symposium, and encouraged me to be creative in approaching the subject matter. Heather Herman, likewise, did a masterful job of making sure everything went as scheduled including an invaluable and impromptu run to purchase wine for an evening dinner. Both Adrienne and Heather tolerated my poor planning with good humor and forbearance.

I also owe thanks to several colleagues. Bob Mann gladly served as a moderator of the discussion, moved the conversation foreword, and offered insights into the discussion. When we realized we needed a chapter that more directly addressed media coverage of polling, Johanna Dunaway stepped up to the plate and quickly wrote an excellent chapter detailing the effects of declining news resources on coverage of polls. Mike Xenos similarly offered his expertise in new media to explore the implications of online opinion expression even as he was under the gun of several other looming deadlines. But perhaps no one played a larger and more sustained role than my graduate assistant, Ashley Kirzinger. Ashley helped to edit each of the essays, offered constructive criticism throughout the process, and even coauthored one of the chapters. Throughout the process, she worked with unusual enthusiasm and good humor. The project would not have been the same without her, nor would it have been as much fun.

My final note of thanks is to my family—Beth, Hannah, and Spencer—who tolerate my workaholic tendencies and help to keep me grounded. Without them, none of this would matter.

INTRODUCTION

The Meaning and Measure of Public Opinion

CHARLIE COOK

Unquestionably, polls in our society and particularly in the world of politics and the media have become both ubiquitous and enormously influential. The combination of technology lowering the once formidable barriers to entry into polling and the increasingly insatiable appetite of cable network news and the Internet for content have driven the proliferation of polls and interest in their results. Simply put, there are so many more polls—good, bad, and, methodologically speaking, ugly—than there used to be. These polls are driving the news and playing an increasingly important role in the national conversation about politics and issues.

It is hard to argue with anything that measures and communicates the public will and helps us understand what that public will is. At the same time, the proliferation of polls and the appetite for their results have created new problems. On the one hand, there are some in the business who are less than fastidious about their methodology, write flawed and slanted questionnaires, or stretch the analysis beyond appropriate parameters. It is not hard to find poll results that seem to serve little purpose other than making news or titillating the public. Even in cases where the question wording is legitimate, far too often the data are misinterpreted or exaggerated, whether consciously to advance a political candidate, party, or ideology or by those who misunderstand the limits of what the data mean or how far a point can be pushed.

On the other hand, there are some enormously dedicated and conscientious professionals who, despite their best efforts and great expense, are having an increasingly difficult time obtaining representative samples with an acceptable response rate, undermining the credibility and reliability of the polling data. Even many of the best in the business will at least privately, and some publicly, concede that they are having to work harder and with a more creative approach to their work in order to keep the quality and dependability of their data at the level of a decade or two ago.

Taken together, the challenges facing both pollsters and users of public opinion research are greater than at any other time in perhaps a half century, all at a time when polling is more influential and ubiquitous than ever before.

These challenges make this volume and the October 2009 Breaux Symposium at Louisiana State University in Baton Rouge, which led to the writing of this book, enormously timely and important. It is not coincidental that this symposium was held at LSU's Manship School of Mass Communication. More than any other mass communication program in the country, the Manship School has focused on the critical intersection of politics and the media, so it is appropriate that it examine closely the challenges in public opinion research for both politics and the media. It is a conversation that badly needed to be held, and this was the right place to have it.

I approach this foreword and the Breaux Symposium at LSU from several perspectives. Having worked as a pollster at Hamilton and Staff, a Democratic polling firm, some thirty years ago, I witnessed the end of the last great transition in survey research: in-person, face-to-face interviewing giving way to person-to-person telephone polling. Only a handful of the most senior pollsters today can recall the wistfulness that accompanied abandoning a methodology that had come to be seen as the industry standard. But the enormous expense of sending out "poll-takers," as the *New York Times* used to call them, became prohibitive, as pollsters fanned out across a state, a district, or the nation interviewing people on their doorsteps, in their living rooms, or around the kitchen table. Questions also began to arise as to whether all of those interviewers were actually going into high-crime urban areas or driving hundreds of miles to reach distant rural respondents.

Once the United States reached near-universal home telephone service, the growing demand of market and public opinion research, the cost savings of having centralized phone banks, and the argument that quality control over the interviewing process was better from phone banks prevailed, and the conversion began.

Since that great transition, mainframes have given way to personal computers, tracking surveys featuring moving averages have become common, focus groups and other qualitative research measures have been employed more, and there have been improvements in sampling, questionnaire construction, and statistical software packages. Still, polling really had not changed much until very recently.

After hanging up my pollster hat and going on to work in politics, I moved over to become a professional consumer of polling data, consulting on and managing campaigns, working on a national party campaign committee, and helping to manage one of the largest trade association political action committees. Twenty-five years ago I transitioned into journalism, writing two weekly political columns and writing and editing a political newsletter that uses and depends on polling data. Now there is hardly a working hour of the day that avoids any use, analysis, or examination of polling data in one form or another.

All of this has made me, I admit, a bit of a snob on the subject. I have come to believe that not all pollsters are equally rigorous in their thinking and their methodologies, nor are they intellectually honest in their analyses or, in a very few cases, honest at all. The vast majority of pollsters strive for excellence, but as in any other line of work, some get there, some get part of the way there, and occasionally some make little attempt to achieve it at all. As a result, aficionados of public opinion research have come to place greater weight on those pollsters with established track records for quality, all the while remembering that even the best are "wrong" about 5 percent of the time, and tend to view the work of newcomers with a healthy dose of skepticism and regard a few others as little more than charlatans.

There are some journalists, bloggers, activists, and others who see "independent" polls, those most often conducted by or for news organizations or colleges and universities, as inherently more reliable, while viewing polls conducted by partisan polling firms, particularly those of the opposite party, as propaganda and not to be believed. This has not been my experience at all. While it is true that campaigns and political parties rarely release polling data that put their candidate or side in an unfavorable light (the release of polling by one side or cause or another is usually self-serving), the survey research commissioned from many of the top firms of either party is typically of higher quality—more sophisticated and methodologically more rigorous—than that produced by all but the very best "independent" firms, namely, Gallup, Pew Research, and the major network/national newspaper partners. Conversely, in light of tighter newsroom and academic budgets, and often less experience and accountability, the "independent" polls are often superficial or less reliable. Generalizations are always dangerous, but my experience has been that most experienced political polling firms produce fewer dubious results than others and that some of those polls sponsored by local news organizations and some in academia are among the worst, often with embarrassingly small sample sizes or faulty, if any, screening for voters, in the case of political campaigns.

Sadly, few consumers of survey research can be discriminating enough to know which pollsters, partisan or independent, are the talented and conscientious, scrupulously honest practitioners of this combination of science and art. They thus tend to either dismiss or believe all polls or, more likely, believe only those polls that support their own personal political point of view.

But even the most talented and conscientious pollsters are facing challenges far greater than those that existed a generation ago. An overzealous and out-of-control telemarketing industry has all but destroyed the willingness of millions of Americans to pick up the phone and cooperate with a public opinion survey. Telemarketers, some even posing as pollsters, too often interrupted people's evening activities: meal preparation, family dinner hours, diaper changing, and homework study periods. This has made it very hard to get completed interviews from a representative sample. Between the invention and widespread use of caller ID and people simply becoming more willing to say "no thanks, I do not want to participate," the world of polling has become far more difficult than it was for pollsters a generation or two ago.[1] During the symposium, Scott Keeter, the director of survey research at the Pew Research Center, pointed to research showing that the average response rates for pollsters between 1996 and 2004 was 30 percent but that in recent years, even with the Pew Research Center's incredibly rigorous efforts, it had dropped to the low 20s and even high teens, a rate of decline of 1 or 2 percentage points per year. This problem alone warrants significant concern about the current and particularly the future reliability of survey research, even among the most conscientious of practitioners.

There is also the coverage issue. The proliferation of cell phones, with more and more people, particularly young people, abandoning the traditional landline telephone, has undermined what had become the mainstay method of gathering survey research, since face-to-face interviewing had been largely abandoned. While increasingly the most conscientious and best-funded pollsters are including cell respondents in their samples, the question of how many should be blended into the larger sample and how they should be weighted is debatable. The same can be said of whether a pollster can use a questionnaire instrument of the same length with a respondent on a cell phone, who may be driving or walking down the street.

Then there is the question of geography. In the old days, a pollster could accurately ascertain where a respondent lived by simply looking at the area code and telephone exchange, the first three digits after the area code. But now, with telephone number and particularly cell phone portability and an increasingly transient population, that respondent may not necessarily live in even the same time zone or part of the country as his or her cell phone area code might suggest. Moreover, new federal laws and regulations and a patchwork of state laws restrict the calling of cell phones, the use of computerized predictive dialers, and other aspects of survey taking.

Finally, with lower voter participation rates, many political pollsters use commercially obtained voter lists with telephone numbers matched for their samples instead of the less expensive but easier random digit dialing method, but the effectiveness of the voter-telephone number match varies enormously.[2]

All of this means that the cost of high-quality, methodologically rigorous survey research has gone sky high, as Democratic pollster Anna Greenberg pointed out at the symposium, ranging from $30 per completion for a random digit dialing interview all the way to as much as $80 each for a cell phone completion. For campaigns and other organizations, particularly news organizations with tighter budgets, the temptation to cut corners and use less conscientious methodologies and low-bid, low-quality vendors is great.

Not surprisingly, the skyrocketing cost of high-quality research along with changes in the nature of polling has opened up the market for new entrants. Virtually anyone can download or purchase survey research tabulation software, purchase a random digit dial sample, and either buy a machine that can make the interactive voice response (IVR) phone calls or subcontract out interviewing to a field service and, voilà, become a pollster. Needless to say, caveat emptor.

Some are pushing Internet polling. Obviously, the costs would be extremely low, making it very appealing. But the limitations on reaching representative samples of low-income, less-educated, and older respondents are huge, and no one has addressed them satisfactorily; nor are they likely to be addressed anytime soon. That is not to say that there is no utility of any form of public opinion research using the Internet. Indeed, at the conference, Anna Greenberg discussed some ways that she and her firm have used the Internet to do some qualitative interest research, not attempting to reach a representative slice of Americans.

IVR polling, also known as robo-polling, is increasingly being used and gradually gaining acceptance, despite reservations among many professionals and consumers of public opinion research about the limitations and reliability of that research. In these IVR surveys, respondents are asked to answer the recorded questions by touching the keys on their telephone. Initially, the purists (myself included) were totally dismissive of the new method. Indeed, one of the participants in the symposium quoted an academic as referring to it as computerized response audience polls (or "CRAP" for short), and even today the quality of IVR polling varies enormously from one pollster to another. The most careful users of this methodology are producing some high-quality data, in some cases almost as accurate as, or even more accurate than, the information obtained by traditional live interviewer pollsters for predicting electoral outcomes. But IVR questionnaires are generally thought to be reliable only if they are relatively brief, limiting the amount of information that a single survey can collect, and some still wonder whether adults or voters are being interviewed in every case.

Simply put, even the best and most conscientious pollsters using live interviewers are facing greater technical challenges than ever before. Tighter budgets promote cutting corners, and there is less differentiation between the results of high-quality polls conducted by experienced professional live interviewers and those conducted using the IVR method. The increasingly high, even prohibitive costs of using traditional methods also drive some users of public opinion research, in their desperation to lower costs, to use less expensive methods and providers—amateurs, rookies, and even charlatans. There was even a 2009 case of a fairly new firm bursting on the scene, doing polls in every corner of the country. The results were cited by television networks and some of the country's leading newspapers, and it now appears that much of the interviewing and results were completely fabricated.

But very few consumers of the media, and even journalists and campaign operatives, are in a position to be discriminating users of survey research. Most are not able to distinguish the good from the bad and to understand the limitations of polls in this ever challenging environment. Many now seem to not trust any polls or believe only those surveys that produce results that corroborate what they would like to see as the truth, an extension of the increasingly polarized nature of the news media today.

At the risk of repetition, the Breaux Symposium and this book make a terrific contribution to shining a light, examining the challenges facing public opinion research and its increased use in politics and the media, advancing a conversation that has largely been conducted just among those in the field and behind closed doors. I hope that a better understanding of the problems will promote a greater appreciation of the use and abuse of data, and the limitations on their reliability, and will advance efforts to address these problems and help promote solutions.

I also hope this conversation will serve as an impetus for journalists, encouraging those covering politics or utilizing survey research to learn more about polling, analyzing, and interpreting data and providing them with at least a rudimentary understanding of statistical analysis, leading them to become more sophisticated in their use of data in their stories. Far too often, political reporters, editors, television producers, talk show hosts, bloggers, and others, with their insatiable appetite for eye-catching and provocative poll results, will abuse numbers or focus on numbers that are often newsworthy only because they are outliers, inconsistent with other results. The outlier does not reflect a new trend finding but rather signifies that the poll or question is simply wrong or flawed. Such "new" findings are gleefully seized upon, the new data sensationalized, even if there is a mountain of data, and even logic, suggesting otherwise.

The proliferation of polls, an insatiable appetite for data, and new challenges facing public opinion research mean that journalists need more than ever to understand polling and survey methods. They must analyze and use the data in an intelligent and responsible way so that their readers, viewers, and listeners benefit from their analysis, instead of being misled by the numbers and the conclusions drawn from the numbers.

NOTES

1. Richard Curtin, Stanley Presser, and Eleanor Singer, "Changes in Telephone Survey Nonresponse over the Past Quarter Century," *Public Opinion Quarterly* 69 (2005): 87–98; Allyson Holbrook, Jon Krosnick, and Alison Pfent, "The Causes and Consequences of Response Rates in Surveys by the News Media and Government Contractor Survey Research Firms," in *Advances in Telephone Survey Methodology,* ed. James M. Lepkowski, N. Clyde Tucker, J. Michael Brick, Edith D. De Leeuw, Lilli Japec, Paul J. Lavrakas, Michael W. Link, and Roberta L. Sangster, 499–528 (New York: Wiley, 2007).

2. For a discussion of the advantages and disadvantages of registration-based sampling, see Donald Green and Alan Gerber, "Improving the Accuracy of Election Forecasts," *Campaigns and Elections* 19 (1998): 51–57; Donald Green and Alan Gerber, "Can Registration-Based Sampling Improve the Accuracy of Midterm Election Forecasts?" *Public Opinion Quarterly* 70 (2006): 197–223. Green and Gerber note the variance in the coverage of registration lists, though they also find that registration-based sampling is more accurate when it comes to predicting election outcomes.

POLITICAL POLLING IN THE DIGITAL AGE

1

Public Opinion Polling in a Digital Age
Meaning and Measurement
KIRBY GOIDEL

Since 1936 when George Gallup bested the *Literary Digest* straw poll, public opinion in American politics has been synonymous with scientifically based opinion polling. Public opinion, in this respect, has been defined primarily as the aggregation of privately held individual opinions as revealed through carefully constructed questions posed to randomly selected samples. Such a definition fit perfectly within the context of the broadcast era of American politics in which information was distributed through a small number of channels (primarily the major networks and daily newspapers) and the opportunities for public feedback were limited. Public opinion was the mass audience, mostly passive and reactive to elite communications. In the 2009 Breaux Symposium, we considered how well this definition of public opinion, as well as its measurement through polling, holds up in a digital age with almost unlimited information choices and opportunities for public feedback. This much is clear: survey research is going through its most significant transition since the development and widespread adoption of probability-based sampling in 1936. What emerges from this transition is likely to differ in important ways from the mainstay of survey research from 1974 to the present—landline telephone interviews based on random digit dialing.

Over the past several years, pollsters have struggled with significant challenges to the credibility of their work, including declining response rates and an increased reliance on cell phones for interpersonal communication.

While it might be an overstatement to suggest that the polling industry is in the midst of a crisis, the credibility of public opinion research has, with good reason, been increasingly called into question. Pollsters have generally confronted these challenges as technical problems with technical solutions. A growing cell-phone-only population, for example, could be addressed by sampling from banks of cell phone numbers or through address-based sampling.

The technical difficulties confronting pollsters may, however, reflect a more interesting possibility: public opinion in a digital age may be more elusive and consequently less easily measured than in the past. In a digital age, aggregating privately held individual opinions may be insufficient to the task of capturing an increasingly dynamic and interactive public. In this respect, the growth and widespread adoption of digital media—the Internet, social networking sites, blogs, Twitter, cell phones, and now smart phones—have increased not only the amount and diversity of information available to citizens but also the opportunities for political participation and opinion expression. The conversation of politics in this environment is ongoing and incomplete and not easily captured in the snapshot of the public mood provided by opinion polls.

This may sound like a narrow distinction, but it is of considerable theoretical and practical importance. In the first instance, the solution is a better telescope, a more refined or precise scientific instrument. Overcome the technical challenges (e.g., dual-frame sampling to capture cell-phone-only and cell-phone-mostly respondents) and the problem is solved. In the second instance, the very nature of the phenomena under study is different, perhaps because the initial theorizing was limited in scope or perhaps because the old definition is no longer tenable under a new reality. Refined instrumentation in the latter instance will not suffice because what is needed is new theorizing (e.g., Einstein theorizing that light is better described as discrete particles as opposed to waves). But if public opinion is indeed more difficult to capture, an important and lingering question is left open: Why are there so many people conducting so many surveys?

The Proliferation of Polls

There can be little question that scientific opinion polling has fundamentally reshaped the American political landscape. Almost every candidate message is carefully pretested to understand which issues and phrases move candidate support. Elected officials and their advisers pore over poll results to guide policy-making decisions. While it is a myth to suggest that politicians blindly follow polls, poll results unquestionably help to shape political agendas and persuasive messages.

Journalists frequently decry this prefabricated poll-tested politics as inauthentic, but they are hardly immune to the influence or pervasiveness of polling. Indeed, they are the leading cause. The horse race is the mainstay of election coverage as news focuses primarily on who is ahead and by how much. Pity the candidate who does not poll well. He or she gets little or no coverage, finds it nearly impossible to raise money, and is often excluded from media-sponsored debates. Pity as well the candidate or elected official who begins falling in the polls (à la Hillary Clinton in the 2008 Democratic primaries). A decline in public support can drive the campaign narrative, as every act and pronouncement is interpreted in light of a faltering campaign or a failed administration. Most of all, pity the candidate who goes off script and makes an "authentic" error. Missteps—even literally falling off a stage—can be the death knell for aspiring candidates with subsequent coverage driving down candidate support and favorability ratings. Politically, it is much safer to avoid the straight talk express (à la John McCain) and stay on script (à la George W. Bush). Leave aside for now the question of whether polls should play such a prominent role in news coverage and consider this instead: Should polls play such a prominent role when the credibility of polling is increasingly in doubt? And do journalists who cover politics have a sufficient understanding of polling to decipher good polling from bad?

When news coverage does briefly turn to the issues, it is generally placed within the broader framework of campaign strategy and gamesmanship.[1] Polling, which could be used to illuminate political issues and public preferences, is instead used as part of an ongoing game in which the news media continuously track who is ahead and who is behind. A new announcement on health care policy, for example, is almost never interpreted as a statement on policy but rather as an effort to shift the campaign agenda onto more favorable turf. Once the campaign is over, news coverage focuses relentlessly on various measures of public approval—from standard presidential approval to more detailed questions on the president's agenda (e.g., health care reform, the economy, and foreign affairs). Virtually every presidential action or policy position is part of an ongoing referendum of randomly selected samples with added commentary from journalists and pundits. For newspapers with declining circulations, revenue, and staff, opinion polls provide an easy story line or narrative to frame political developments and breaking events.

Nor is the impact of polling limited to politics. Nearly every aspect of human behavior has been the subject of a survey question and subsequent data analysis. Market researchers examine the odds of various purchasing decisions, lump consumers into segments (or clusters) based on buying patterns and lifestyle preferences, and target persuasive messages accordingly. In the political realm, these segments become popularized as soccer moms, security moms, Bubbas, and NASCAR dads and the focus of targeted communications designed to mobilize the political base or persuade cross-pressured voters.

Polls are so pervasive that the sheer number of polls is thought to be a major contributor in driving down survey response. While it is difficult to get exact estimates on the number of polling organizations or the number of polls conducted, Figure 1.1 presents the number of marketing research and public opinion firms as reflected in Census Bureau economic data. Missing from the data are academic survey research centers and polling services provided within larger organizations where survey research is not the primary financial activity. These limitations aside, the trend should be apparent: the number of polling firms and the level of polling activity have increased continuously at least since 1997.

Given the sheer volume of polling and upward trend in activity, it might be surprising to learn that the pollsters have been struggling with challenges to the credibility of their work. First, the *public* polls purport to measure is increasingly hard to reach as potential respondents rely on technology (e.g., caller ID and answering machines) to screen or block calls from unknown numbers. Wary of telemarketing calls and push polls, they are also less inclined to cooperate when contacted. As a result, reported response rates have declined precipitously over the past several decades to the point where only a quarter of respondents answer the typical telephone survey. Response rates are even lower (often in the single digits) for overnight polls designed to gauge public reactions to political events, presidential speeches, or political debates. Existing research indicates that low response rates may be less of a problem than often feared as nonrespondents do not often deviate sub-

Figure 1.1. Total Marketing Research and Public Opinion and Polling Establishments

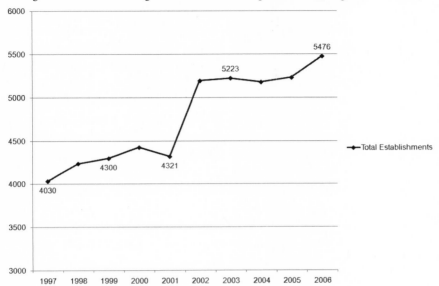

stantially from respondents in most surveys, particularly after appropriate poststratification weights are applied to the data.[2] Even so, the potential for response bias is a serious concern, and the degree to which it affects the results of any given survey is generally an unknown.

Perhaps the more pressing challenge to pollsters has been a growing reliance on cell phones for interpersonal communication. According to some estimates, landline telephone surveys may miss as much as 30 percent of the population—including individuals who have abandoned landline telephones altogether (the cell-only population) and individuals who still have landline phones but rarely or never use them (the cell-mostly population).

Collectively, the challenges confronting survey research and the continued growth of public opinion polling present something of a paradox. Pollsters are increasingly confronting serious challenges to the quality of their data, addressing these challenges increases the costs of conducting survey research, and yet the demand for polling—and the supply of pollsters—have only increased over time. Covering the economics of the polling industry is beyond the scope of the current analysis, but two points are important within this context:

1. *Lower barriers, rising costs.* The barriers to entering the polling industry have declined significantly over the past decade. Even within the context of traditional landline telephone surveys, software for data collection (CATI) and data analysis (e.g., SPSS, STATA, and SAS) has become more affordable and user-friendly. Automated telephone surveys, also referred to as robo-polls (but more appropriately called interactive voice response, or IVR, polls), make it possible to conduct surveys without the added costs of telephone interviewers. IVR polls do about as well as traditional telephone surveys in predicting the winner of an election, but they provide little or no contextual understanding of campaigns or issues. The situation with Web surveys is even worse: "Essential tools of political polling," David Hill observed, "are more accessible to the untrained than ever. Online services like SurveyMonkey (an apt label) will probably accelerate the slide of the industry. A clear majority of pollsters today has no formal academic training in the trade."[3] Creating and conducting online polls is easier than ever, requiring little or no understanding of survey research, questionnaire construction, or statistics. Ease of entry also increases the possibility of outright fraud as highlighted by recent allegations of data fabrication. In separate incidents, Strategic Vision and Research 2000 were accused of fabricating data after statistical analyses revealed highly unlikely patterns in the reported results.[4] Despite lower barriers to entry, however, the costs of doing quality, rigorous opinion polling have increased substantially. Declining response rates have increased the costs of contacting respondents, as each completed interview requires more time, effort, and money. And while sampling cell phone numbers increases the coverage of surveys, it adds significantly to the overall costs. According to most estimates, cell phone surveys costs three to five times as much as comparable landline surveys.

2. *Economic value of survey data.* Surveys generally use probability-based sampling to estimate candidate or issue support within a larger population, but carefully constructed surveys may also help political professionals identify which issues and phrases move candidate support and which groups of voters to target with specific

campaign appeals. Understanding variations due to question wording, for example, helps to effectively frame candidate issue positions. Survey findings may prove less representative of the overall population but may still be valuable if they help to identify issues that move candidate favorability ratings or the best language to frame a given message. Despite the challenges, the economic value of survey data appears undiminished and indeed may have grown as candidates look to reduce the uncertainty of the electoral process and as journalists and political analysts look to provide a contextual understanding of the campaign process.

The result of this economic context is a proliferation in polling but wide variance in the quality of the work. Given this situation, it should come as little surprise that professional organizations (e.g., the American Association of Public Opinion Research) are placing a renewed emphasis on standards—or that blogs and Web sites, such as Pollster.com, have arisen as watchdogs over polling practices and to help provide a better contextual understanding of poll results.

Yet for all the important work being done to assure the credibility of poll results, the question remains whether it is enough. Is the very best polling—with sophisticated sampling strategies and nuanced and careful data analysis—sufficient to capture the meaning of public opinion in a digital age? Or do we need to rethink the meaning of public opinion in contemporary politics? Inherent in these questions is the idea that the meaning of public opinion and its role in American politics have changed over time. In providing an answer, we assume public opinion does (and should) matter in democratic governance but leave open questions of how public opinion is expressed and how, when, and to what effect public opinion is recognized and acted upon by policymakers.

Political Context and the Meaning of Public Opinion

To James Madison, public opinion was indispensable to a republican form of government but would cause great harm to individual rights and liberties if left unchecked. "Had every Athenian been a Socrates," Madison writes in

The Federalist Papers No. 55, "every Athenian assembly would still have been a mob." The institutional framework crafted by the U.S. Constitution is a testament to Madison's concerns about the potentially adverse consequences of government by the people.

The larger contours of American political history have witnessed the expansion of "the public" to groups originally excluded from political participation (poor white males, African Americans, and women) and the opening of channels for greater direct public influence over elected officials (e.g., the direct election of U.S. senators established by the Seventeenth Amendment and the adoption of direct primaries). As the definition of the public expanded and channels for public influence increased, the expression of public opinion narrowed to focus first on counting votes and then on the expression of privately held opinions as measured through the public opinion poll.

Over time, the primary tool for gauging public opinion—the public opinion poll—became synonymous with the definition of public opinion and served as one of the central mechanisms for public feedback and influence over the policy-making processes. If this seems obvious, one might contrast the definition with the one offered by V. O. Key Jr., "as opinions held by private persons which governments find it useful to heed" or Rousseau's more amorphous conceptualization of the general will.[5] Regardless, since 1936, the scientific construction of public opinion dominated public discourse and social science research. As Leo Bogart observed in 1985: "The world of public opinion in today's sense really began with the Gallup polls of the mid-1930s and it is impossible for us to retreat to the meaning of public opinion as it was understood by Thomas Jefferson in the eighteenth century, by Alexis de Tocqueville and Lord Bryce in the nineteenth,—or even Walter Lippmann in 1922."[6] One may fairly argue that survey research during this period achieved paradigm status in the social sciences, focusing research on "normal science" problems that could be solved through standardized questionnaires and random sampling. There is little question survey research came to dominate public discourse about public opinion, its meaning, and its influence over the political process.

Not that the preeminence of polling went unchallenged or the shortcomings unnoticed. Early academic research indicated a public largely unaffected by political campaigns and instead heavily influenced by partisan attachments learned through early childhood socialization.[7] Research examining the nature of mass belief systems diagnosed the public as poorly informed and lacking stable beliefs or ideological structure.[8] While subsequent research demonstrated a public that does relatively well with limited information,[9] none of this work has fundamentally dispelled the portrait of the typical citizen as uninformed and often holding contradictory and ambivalent attitudes on even the most visible and emotionally laden issues. V. O. Key Jr. famously declared that the "voters are not fools,"[10] but—as decades of survey research reveal—nor are they ideal citizens.

The failure of citizens to meet the norms of classic liberal democratic theory haunted survey research. Can a mostly disinterested public have meaningful opinions on technically complex issues, such as embryonic stem cell research, global warming, or the financial meltdown in 2008? Or are poll responses mostly nonopinions masquerading as meaningful public engagement?[11]

Proponents of deliberative democracy further criticize polling for capturing what public opinion is, rather than what it might be after thoughtful discussion and consideration of the issues.[12] More broadly, polling was criticized for implicitly crafting a passive form of citizenship whereby opinion was defined as aggregated totals of privately held beliefs.[13] The role of the public and the public sphere, in this view, was limited to expressing satisfaction or dissatisfaction with elected officials or policy decisions. The daily tracking of presidential approval ratings, for example, can be seen as akin to Nielsen ratings for television programming, an important but limited form of political communication and influence.

Despite such criticisms, public opinion polling emerged as the dominant form for representing collective preferences from 1936 onward because it was more structured, more scientific, and *more democratic* than other forms of opinion expression. Scientifically valid survey research, George Gallup argued, allowed for the expression of public opinion without the intermediaries of interest groups and political parties and reflected a truer representation of public opinion than other forms of communication. Archibald Crossley similarly observed in 1937: "Scientific polling makes it possible within two or three days at moderate expense for the entire nation to work hand in hand with its legislative representatives, on laws which affect our daily lives. Here is the long-sought key to 'Government by the people.'"[14]

The emergence of public opinion polling—not surprisingly—coincided with the development and widespread diffusion of the broadcast media and the development of a mass culture through radio, television, and film.[15] In this respect, the opinion poll served as the perfect complement to a media system in which information is disseminated through a limited number of channels to mass audiences. The social construction of the public as an aggregated total of individual opinions in such an environment served the very real and useful purpose of summarizing political attitudes and behaviors, as well as market-related choices and behaviors. The link between political uses of survey research methods and the need to understand mass markets and mass audiences is inescapable. Jean Converse's definitive and exhaustive history of survey research, for example, notes that public opinion polls borrowed heavily from existing market research. "The famous trio of Gallup, Roper, and Crossley constructed the new opinion polls in a merger of the two fields, using methods of market research and financing them with the money and publicity of election straw-vote journalism."[16]

This leads us to a relatively straightforward proposition. Public opinion polling, as it is conventionally constructed and practiced, is most useful within media systems dominated by broadcast media. During the broadcast era, it was easy to imagine an identifiable "public" as constructed by exposure to similar news sources and political messages and as measured in public opinion polls as statistical aggregates. Take the case of a presidential address. Prior to the advent of cable, the vast majority of Americans would have watched the address on one of the three broadcast networks as the speech was actually being delivered.[17] Today, citizens might watch the address or switch to HBO, MTV, or some other cable channel. Alternatively, they might watch the entire speech in real time, watch later on their DVR, or watch selected clips on YouTube or on *The Daily Show with Jon Stewart.*

If exposure to information was more uniform during the broadcast era, the avenues for public participation were constrained by a limited number of access points to express political viewpoints and relatively static media choices. Citizens had a limited ability to "talk back" to the news through letters to the editor but almost no opportunity to create their own content. Democracy in this period might be best conceptualized as broad but not particularly deep with the "public" defined as relatively passive consumers of information and "public opinion" defined generally as privately held preferences. In classic communication models, the feedback loop for political messages and news content was not particularly well developed. When it did function, it operated as a blunt instrument.

Contemporary politics, in contrast, are increasingly defined by interactivity, increased access points for participation, and virtual communities. Not only do citizens have a greater opportunity to respond to political content directly, but they can also alter, edit, and forward existing content or create and post original content of their own. Given the shortcomings of the broadcast era, this might seem like a democratic panacea, but all change comes with associated costs. With greater choice, politically disinterested citizens attend to less political news and more partisan news sources (e.g., Fox News, MSNBC, and partisan political blogs), expanding the knowledge gap and further polarizing the electorate.[18] Moreover, digital media may enhance political participation, but the renewed democratic impulse is decidedly pluralistic in form and content. If public opinion polling was once criticized for constructing the public as a statistical aggregate, public opinion in a digital media age is decidedly fragmented and disaggregated.[19]

For present purposes, we raise a slightly different question: How does a changing media system challenge the measurement and interpretation of public opinion? Can we meaningfully speak of "a public" during an era of personalized communications and social networking? In many ways, this is not a new question, as public opinion scholars have long noted the importance of the various dimensions of public opinion—distribution, stability, intensity, and salience—in interpreting survey results and the existence and importance of issue publics. Indeed, most classes on public opinion (or American government) quickly dismiss the unrealistic assumptions of classic democratic theory or models of majoritarian democracy, opting instead to discuss the tenets of pluralism and the importance of public representation through political parties, interest groups, and social movements. In this respect, public opinion has been widely recognized as a misnomer in that it reflects not a single public but multiple publics whose attention and interest shift with the issue at hand.

These old questions, however, are given a new wrinkle by a communication revolution that has transformed and redefined contemporary politics. Not since the advent of the printing press has technology—the Internet, cell phones, and social networking sites—so thoroughly redefined the political landscape. For the moment, we remain agnostic about the net effects of these changes and instead simply raise a set of questions: Have digital technologies provided the seed or realization of a democratic resurgence? Have they deepened existing chasms between haves and have-nots, expanding the digital divide and leaving a political process that sings more strongly than ever with an "upper-class accent?"[20] Information is more plentiful than ever, but is the public better informed or is it increasingly lost in the "great, blooming, buzzing confusion?"[21] More important for our purposes, has digital technology made polling less useful as mechanism for understanding public opinion?

Public opinion polling will never be obsolete. The form of polling, however, may be undergoing a revolutionary transformation, and political professionals may find an increasing need to supplement polling with other forms of richer, more contextualized data. Two historic parallels are particularly instructive: (1) 1936, when the failure of *Literary Digest* ushered in the modern era of scientific opinion polling; and (2) 1974, the year often cited as the beginning of the gradual acceptance of telephone surveys as a cost-effective substitute for face-to-face interviews.[22] It is perhaps worth noting that telephone interviews were initially dismissed, especially by academics, as yielding lower-quality data and poor coverage of the general population. "We adopted the telephone method in the 1970s," Don Dillman writes, "not because it was inherently better than face-to-face interviews, but because it was cheaper. Self-administered modes such as the Internet and IVR are being adopted not because they are inherently better for obtaining answers but rather because the cost factors are advantageous."[23] It is unclear whether 1936 or 1974 is the better analogy for contemporary polling, but there is little question that our understanding of public opinion—both its meaning and its measurement—is changing in important and lasting ways.

To begin to understand the meaning of public opinion in contemporary politics, we start this volume with an assessment of the measurement of public opinion by means of the public opinion poll. Perhaps no single organization has been more innovative in addressing the technical challenges confronting survey research than the Pew Center for the People & the Press. And few scholars can explain these challenges and the ongoing efforts to address them as well as Scott Keeter, director of survey research at the Pew Center. In Chapter 2, Keeter provides an overview of contemporary polling, assessing the challenges of growing survey nonresponse and cell-phone-only and cell-phone-mostly populations. On reading the chapter, it is hard not to be taken back by both the severity of the problems and the concerted effort of the polling industry to address them. Unlike in 1936, there is a remarkable openness to experimenting with new methods and approaches to understanding the meaning of public opinion and an ongoing commitment to the idea that opinion polling can enhance democratic politics by giving voice to collective preferences. As Keeter concludes:

> Our faith that polling's problems will find a solution rests less with any particular technological innovation, mathematical method or new database than with the conviction that human beings remain interested in the world around them and fundamentally amenable to offering their perspective and reactions to strangers who ask.

If the measurement of public opinion remains viable despite considerable concerns, the growth in the number of polls combined with substantial variance in methodological approaches across polling organizations raises a related but different issue: How can citizens, journalists, and political elites know which polls to trust? Answering this question is the task Mark Blumenthal takes on in Chapter 3. Blumenthal writes the Mystery Pollster column for the *National Journal* and is the cofounder of Pollster.com. He notes that industry standards as to what constitutes a good poll have changed drastically in recent years. IVR polls, for example, have been shown to be reasonably accurate in predicting elections, while survey nonresponse has proven to be less problematic than once feared. With the field in transition, a set of "best practices" or industry standards is likely to remain elusive. A commitment to transparency in reporting poll results, however, not only is obtainable but would also provide citizens, journalists, and political elites with valuable information about the trustworthiness of individual polls and polling organizations. The call for transparency is made more urgent by recent allegations and compelling statistical evidence that pollsters Strategic Vision and R2000 may have passed off fabricated poll results as scientific research.

The construction of public opinion does not occur through measurement alone. Indeed, poll numbers are most often given meaning not by pollsters but by journalists in the tone and framing of political news coverage. Journalists, after all, define the campaign narrative and map the contours of policy debates. As Johanna Dunaway observes, these narratives are often driven by poll results. In Chapter 4, Dunaway examines news coverage of public opinion polls, documenting how the decline in the amount of resources devoted to political news has affected the use of polls to frame political news stories. The findings raise serious normative concerns about how cutbacks in newsrooms led to less substantive, poll-driven news. At a time when the polling industry is transitioning into a new era and grappling with the issues related to standards, journalistic reliance on polls to frame and structure news coverage presents an interesting and troubling paradox. More to the point, even if the pollsters get public opinion right, the meaning may be lost as poll results are translated into news stories. As Mark Blumenthal notes, the most common polling errors are not in coverage, nonresponse, or measurement but in interpretation.

Missing from these analyses is a more fundamental question about the meaning of public opinion in a digital age. Susan Herbst, for example, has long argued that public opinion polls define public opinion too narrowly, capturing the aggregation of privately held beliefs but missing the public conversation about politics and policy. In Chapter 5, she reconsiders this thesis in light of an increasingly interactive information environment and challenges pollsters to go beyond methodological tweaking in assessing political talk as public opinion. Now more than ever, new media technologies provide insight into a public opinion that is more dynamic, interactive, and conversational and in doing so provide insight into the movement and flow of political ideas.

But if political talk is more accessible than ever before, what meaning can we extract from it? In Chapter 6, Kirby Goidel, Ashley Kirzinger, and Mike Xenos consider the nature of online political expression and conclude that online political talk is like other forms of political participation. Expression comes most often from the most intensely partisan voices, is generally directed at "friends" by means of social networking sites and e-mail, and frequently involves forwarding news stories and editorials rather than expressing original thoughts or new ideas. Defining public opinion through online political conversation misses an important ingredient of public opinion—the moderate voter, less certain of his or her beliefs and less willing to offer an unsolicited opinion in a public forum. The public opinion poll, for all its shortcomings, continues to be critical for capturing moderate voices. Even so, there is little question that online expression has greater reach, more immediacy, and fewer filters than traditional communication. And much of this communication is public, meaning that the contours of this public conversation are available for analysis.

In Chapter 7, professional pollster Anna Greenberg explores alternatives to polling, including micro-targeting and online experiments and focus groups. Her work is instructive as a reminder that political professionals are already mining available data for strategic and actionable political information. Even without the costs of cell phones, traditional polling is an increasingly expensive operation, available to only the best-funded political campaigns. And even with limitations, online resources provide potentially cost-effective means for collecting data. For political professionals, Greenberg argues, public opinion data will be increasingly supplemented with other modes of gauging existing public sentiments and understanding how these sentiments might shift with new information.

The book concludes with reflections on the normative value of public opinion in democratic governance as well as the market value of "real-time" polling data. Polls continue to play a pervasive role in American politics because they provide candidates, policymakers, journalists, and bloggers with valuable contextual and strategic information. Polls drive the campaign narrative, guide strategic political decisions, and help translate public preferences into policy. Even so, polling is undergoing its most important methodological shift since the telephone interview replaced face-to-face interviews in the 1970s. This shift, however, is not just about methodology but instead reflects our understanding of the meaning of public opinion in a digital age.

NOTES

1. Thomas Patterson, *Out of Order* (New York: Knopf, 1993).

2. Richard Curtin, Stanley Presser, and Eleanor Singer, "The Effect of Response Rate

Changes on the Index of Consumer Sentiment," *Public Opinion Quarterly* 64 (2000): 413–28; Scott Keeter, Courtney Kennedy, Michael Dimock, Jonathan Best, and Peyton Craighill, "Gauging the Impact of Growing Nonresponse on a National RDD Telephone Survey," *Public Opinion Quarterly* 70 (2006): 759–79.

3. David Hill, "More Poll Police May Be Needed," TheHill.com, February 10, 2009, www.thehill.com/opinion/columnists/david-hill/8438-more-poll-police-may-be-needed (accessed May 29, 2009).

4. Nate Silver, "Strategic Vision Polls Exhibit Unusual Patterns, Possibly Indicating Fraud," www.fivethirtyeight.com/2009/09/strategic-vision-polls-exhibit-unusual.html (accessed July 17, 2010); Daily Kos, "More on Research 2000," June 29, 2010, www.dailykos.com/story/2010/6/29/880185/-More-on-Research-2000 (accessed July 22, 2010).

5. V. O. Key Jr., *Public Opinion and American Democracy* (New York: Knopf, 1961), 14. Jean-Jacques Rousseau, *On the Social Contract*, trans. Roger Masters and Judith Masters (New York: St. Martin's, 1978).

6. Leo Bogart, *Polls and the Awareness of Public Opinion* (New Brunswick, NJ: Transaction Books, 1985), 14.

7. Angus Campbell, Philip Converse, Warren Miller, and Donald Stokes, *The American Voter* (New York: Wiley, 1960).

8. Philip Converse, "The Nature of Belief Systems in the Mass Public," in *Ideology and Discontent*, ed. David Apter (New York: Free Press, 1964).

9. Arthur Lupia and Matthew McCubbins, *The Democratic Dilemma: Can Citizens Learn What They Need to Know?* (Cambridge: Cambridge University Press, 1998); Samuel Popkin, *The Reasoning Voter: Communication and Persuasion in Presidential Campaigns* (Chicago: University of Chicago Press, 1991).

10. V. O. Key Jr., *The Responsible Electorate: Rationality and Presidential Voting, 1936–1960* (Cambridge, MA: Belknap Press, 1966), 7.

11. David Moore, *The Opinion Makers: An Insider Exposes the Truth behind the Polls* (Boston: Beacon Press, 2008); Herbert Asher, *Polling and the Public: What Every Citizen Should Know* (Washington, DC: CQ Press, 2007).

12. James Fishkin, *Democracy and Deliberation: New Directions for Democratic Reform* (New Haven: Yale University Press, 1991); Daniel Yankelovich, *Coming to Public Judgment: Making Democracy Work in a Complex World* (Syracuse, NY: Syracuse University Press, 1991); Scott Althaus, *Collective Preferences in Democratic Politics: Opinion Surveys and the Will of the People* (Cambridge: Cambridge University Press, 2003).

13. Susan Herbst, *Numbered Voices: How Opinion Polling Has Shaped American Politics* (Chicago: University of Chicago Press, 1993); Susan Herbst, *Politics at the Margin: Historical Studies of Public Expression outside the Mainstream* (Cambridge: Cambridge University Press, 1994).

14. Archibald Crossley, "Straw Polls in 1936," *Public Opinion Quarterly* 1 (1937): 24–35, 35.

15. Sarah Igo, *The Averaged American: Surveys, Citizens, and the Making of a Mass Public* (Cambridge, MA: Harvard University Press, 2007).

16. Jean Converse, *Survey Research in the United States: Roots and Emergence* (Berkeley: University of California Press, 1986), 88.

17. Garry Young and William Perkins, "Presidential Rhetoric, the Public Agenda, and the End of Presidential Television's Golden Age," *Journal of Politics* 67 (2005): 1190–1205.

18. Markus Prior, *Post-Broadcast Democracy: How Media Choice Increases Inequality in Political Involvement and Polarizes Elections* (New York: Cambridge University Press, 2007); Shanto Iyengar and Kyu Hahn, "Red Media, Blue Media: Evidence of Ideological Selectivity in Media Use," *Journal of Communication* 59 (2009): 19–39.

19. Sarah Igo concludes in her provocative book *The Averaged American* that just as early survey research helped to define public opinion as statistical aggregate, subsequent research helped to create segmented audiences such as soccer moms or NASCAR dads.

20. E. E. Schattsneider, *The Semi-Sovereign People* (New York: Holt, Rinehart, and Winston, 1960), 34.

21. William James, *Principles of Psychology* (New York: H. Holt and Co., 1890), 488.

22. Telephone surveys were common, but their acceptance for academic work is often connected to Seymour Sudman's declaration in 1974 that telephone interviews could be used for health surveys at the Health Survey Methods Conference. See Don Dillman, "Presidential Address: Navigating the Rapids of Change: Some Observations on Survey Methodology in the Early Twenty-first Century," *Public Opinion Quarterly* 66 (2002): 473–94, 475.

23. Dillman, "Presidential Address: Navigating the Rapids of Change," 482.

2

Public Opinion Polling and Its Problems

SCOTT KEETER

When the news broke on January 21, 1998, that President Bill Clinton might have had an affair with a White House intern, there was a nearly unanimous judgment among the pundit class that, if the allegations were true, Clinton would be forced from office. The public, it was said, would not accept his behavior. Shortly thereafter the first public opinion polls appeared, showing that while majorities of the public disapproved of the president's behavior, majorities also believed that he should not resign or be impeached for taking part in an affair and lying about it. It is very likely that opinion polling saved Bill Clinton's presidency.

For whatever their flaws as an embodiment of public opinion, polls should, at the very least, do what they did in January 1998: provide responses from an accurate and unbiased sample of the public, and not just from those with the strongest emotions and the loudest voices. As Harvard political scientist Sidney Verba observed a few years earlier: "Surveys produce just what democracy is supposed to produce—equal representation of all citizens. The sample survey is rigorously egalitarian; it is designed so that each citizen has an equal chance to participate and an equal voice when participating."[1]

But polling's ability to live up to this ideal is imperiled by a wide range of political, social, and technological trends that have made it more difficult to reach and interview an unbiased and representative sample of Americans. This chapter describes the challenges facing public opinion polling and offers an assessment of the future for polls.

The presidential election of 2008 also posed problems for polls specific to the circumstances of an election featuring an African American nominee and a highly polarized political climate. Yet despite the anxieties of many pollsters, preelection surveys performed well. Nearly all national polls' forecasts came very close to the margin of victory for Barack Obama, and most state polls accurately predicted both the presidential and state-level contests.[2] Of course, election polling is just one of the many ways in which polls are important in our political system, and there may be problems elsewhere that do not afflict election polls. But election polling provides us with a valuable "canary in the coal mine." Election polls provide a unique and highly visible validation of the accuracy of survey research, and polling passed its critical tests in 2008. But the final exam rolls around every two or four years, and some pollsters fear that 2008 may be the end of an era, unless the craft finds a way to adapt to a changing environment.[3]

Fortunately, much of the polling community is well aware of the challenges and is actively working to respond to them. Despite competitive pressures, there is a great degree of openness in the polling community that has led to sharing of methods and insights. Professional organizations of survey researchers, such as the American Association for Public Opinion Research and the Marketing Research Association, have focused on solving problems and improving the craft. Professional journals devote significant space—in the case of *Public Opinion Quarterly,* half or more—to methodological topics. There also has been an emphasis on standards and ethics to ensure that survey research treats respondents well and does not overstate what it can accomplish for its clientele.

Polling's problems are legion. Virtually all political polling is conducted by telephone, and many of the problems polling faces, though by no means all, are specific to that survey mode, most notable the fact that more than one in five households cannot be reached on a landline because more people have chosen to have only a cell phone. Pollsters are increasingly including cell phone samples in their studies, but this entails significant costs and technical challenges. Moreover, nonresponse and other problems faced by landline surveys afflict cell phone samples as well.

Alternative survey modes exist. For much of its history, opinion polling was conducted in person with face-to-face interviews. Some polling still is. But the costs of such interviewing make it impractical for all but most specialized or important studies. Use of the Internet for polling is growing rapidly and holds great promise. But the Internet reaches a smaller percentage of the public than the landline telephone, and even for those theoretically reachable by it, the challenges of obtaining a representative sample remain daunting. Mail surveys—some of which employ address-based sampling (ABS) to ensure coverage of virtually the entire population—are attracting renewed attention as a cost-effective means of reaching most households, but they lack the speed usually needed by contemporary political polls. Many believe that one answer to polling's problems will be the use of mixed-mode approaches that take advantage of the comparative strengths of different ways of sampling and reaching the population.

Larger social trends also are affecting polling's ability to reach and interview random samples of the public. Changes in lifestyle patterns are making it more difficult to find people at home or free to participate in a survey. Telemarketing, solicitations, and automated telephone messaging campaigns bring an ever increasing volume of unexpected calling to the typical household and make it harder for legitimate survey research to reach a willing respondent. And concerns about identity theft and fraud may make people less amenable to an interview. These social factors are occurring in tandem with technological changes that make it easier to block or ignore calls from unknown sources. In light of all these changes, some might consider it surprising that polling still works as well as it does.

Despite all the problems that modern survey research faces, much of it continues to produce a valid, if imperfect, model of the population. As described below, the polling profession is adapting to the challenges and is experimenting with new ways of reaching and interviewing the public. The way forward is not clear, but there may be a way.

The Challenges
Growing Nonresponse

The problem of growing nonresponse is not limited to political polling, of course. Response rates to all types of surveys and survey modes have been declining for decades, both here in the United States and abroad. Surveys conducted by or on behalf of the federal government still get relatively high response rates, and those conducted in person (such as the Current Population Survey) can still exceed 90 percent.[4] But telephone surveys fare much worse. The decline in response rates has been substantial, and there are indications that the rate of decline has accelerated in recent years.[5]

Many academics and others whose understanding of survey research was shaped by college textbooks on research methods or examples from studies such as the General Social Survey are surprised to discover that the typical telephone survey by major polling organizations falls far below their expectation. A review of response rates by media pollsters and government contractor survey firms between 1996 and 2004 found that the average response rate was 30 percent, with media polls somewhat lower and government contractor surveys somewhat higher. Response rates for Pew Research Center surveys, which are typical of those conducted by the major news organizations, now average in the mid- to upper teens, with some studies reaching the mid-20s. Pew Research's response rates have been declining by approximately 2 percentage points per year since the mid-1990s, a rate similar to that documented in other telephone surveys.[6]

But the key determinant of bias is whether the propensity to respond to a survey is correlated with important variables of interest. For example, if Republicans and Democrats are equally difficult to locate and persuade to participate, the poll will not be biased in its estimate of how many of each group there are in the population—even if the response rate is low. However, if Republicans are less willing than Democrats to take part, the survey may incorrectly overstate the proportion of Democrats in the population—even if the response rate is relatively high. This is precisely the concern that many conservatives have expressed about polling. This point of view holds that conservatives are more suspicious of mainstream media organizations, which sponsor many of the national public polls, and thus may decline to take part in them for that reason. The accuracy of preelection telephone polls in recent elections strongly suggests that this view is mistaken.[7]

A great deal of empirical research over the past decade has shown that higher response rates are not associated with greater accuracy in surveys. Two Pew Research Center studies compared surveys conducted with Pew's standard methodology and surveys conducted with a rigorous design that achieved a much higher response rate. In both, the differences between the standard and rigorous results were very modest.[8] A similar study with the University of Michigan Consumer Sentiment Index reached the same conclusion.[9] The response rate is not a reliable guide to the validity of a survey. But it is reasonable to ask how far this principle can be taken. Many public and political surveys already have response rates in the single digits.

Important instances of nonresponse bias have occurred in recent years. The in-person exit polls conducted by the National Election Pool (the major networks and the Associated Press) have experienced differential nonresponse by party affiliation. In both 2004 and 2006, a comparison of precinct-level votes and exit polls in the same precincts shows that in some states Democratic voters were more likely than Republican voters to consent to an interview. This bias did not lead to errors in the exit poll reports. The NEP adjusted for this propensity in estimates provided early on election night and in its final estimates, which were weighted by the vote. But the bias was a source of concern. The absence of a bias in telephone surveys, compared with the bias in exit polls, suggests that the political context of the voting experience led Republicans to be less likely to respond. Demographic factors that are correlated with political preferences may also play a role. Younger voters are more likely than older ones to consent to an exit poll interview, and age was a strong correlate of voter preference in recent elections. Joe Lenski, who managed the exit poll operation for Edison Media Research, observed that "exit poll inaccuracy tends to happen in very partisan, very polarized, very active electorate races," which characterized the elections in 2004, 2006, and 2008.[10]

There also is evidence that nonresponse bias can occur on variables related to social integration, such as volunteer activity.[11] People who are better integrated into their communities are more likely to take part in volunteer work and also more likely to participate in a survey. This means that surveys may overestimate the actual levels of volunteer activity in a population. Similarly, people more interested in politics are more likely to agree to an interview about politics, leading to a potential overestimate of the level of political engagement, political knowledge, or news consumption. The size of most of these biases tends to be relatively small, but they are real.

Research methods textbooks often claim that response rates are crucial indicators of the usefulness of data and sometimes even specify minimally acceptable rates far above the ones typical media surveys now obtain. This perspective is not an isolated one.

This is not to say that nonresponse is not a problem in surveys or that response rates are irrelevant. The potential for bias is greater when there is more nonresponse. And declining response rates mean, at a minimum, that survey organizations must put greater and greater effort into obtaining a sample. In survey research, as in much else, resources expended on one aspect are not available for other uses that might be desirable, such as expanding the sample size, lengthening the survey, testing new questions, or improving the distribution of findings.

Growing Noncoverage

Survey research enjoyed a long period in which personal interviewing of national samples of households was feasible and economical. Telephone penetration was far below 100 percent, and long-distance calling was very expensive. By the 1960s the situation was beginning to change as labor costs for personal interviewing were beginning to rise. But a significant minority of households continued to have no telephone or shared service with other households.

In the United States today, the percentage of households having a land-line telephone (about 74%) is actually slightly lower than it was in 1963 (78 percent).[12] In 1963, the remainder could not be reached by telephone. Today the situation is different. Most of the nonlandline households have at least one adult with a cell phone. About 2 percent still have no telephone service at all, according to the National Health Interview Survey.[13] This presents a problem for survey research but also an opportunity. Far fewer of the least affluent households are unreachable by telephone than was the case even twenty years ago. They are just not reachable by landline.

As with nonresponse, telephone noncoverage might pose little concern if the kinds of people unreachable by landline were similar to those who can be reached. But this is decidedly not the case. In particular, cell-only status is much higher among the young, the poor, and racial minorities. Figure 2.1 shows the percentage of adults in different demographic groups living in

Figure 2.1. Percent Cell-Only

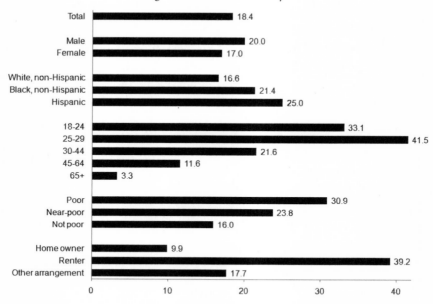

cell-only households, as reported by the National Health Interview Survey for the second half of 2008. (Cell-only status has been growing steadily for the past several years and is undoubtedly higher for all these groups now than is shown in the graph.) More than 40 percent of young adults 25–29 are cell-only, as are one-third of those 18–24. One-quarter of Hispanics are cell-only, and 31 percent of people at or below the federal poverty level are as well. These demographic characteristics are strongly correlated with political preferences, and this relationship is clearly evident in the preferences of landline and cell-only voters in the 2008 national exit poll, which included a question about household telephone status (as did the 2004 exit poll).

About 60 percent of cell-only voters (who constituted 20 percent of all Election Day voters) chose Barack Obama, compared with about 50 percent of the landline-accessible electorate (Table 2.1). Voters with landline service divided nearly evenly between Obama and McCain (50–49 percent). Voters who reported no telephone service were similar to the cell-only group. Given the size of the cell-only population and the sizable political differences between that group and the landline population, the potential for bias in landline surveys is considerable. Because of this concern, many polling or-

Table 2.1.

Presidential Vote by Household Telephone Status in Election Day Exit Polls

	2008		2004	
	Obama (%)	McCain (%)	Kerry (%)	Bush (%)
Popular vote (Election Day + early)	52.9	45.7	48.3	50.7
All Election Day voters	52.4	46.2	48.4	50.8
Landline service	49.7	48.7	47.7	51.4
Only cell phone service	60.5	37.8	53.5	44.4
No telephone service at home	61.1	36.2	58.8	39.5

Sources: Election Day exit polls conducted by National Election Pool, November 4, 2009, and November 2, 2004; Federal Election Commission.

ganizations included cell phone samples in their 2008 preelection polling.[14]

Fortunately, the potential for significant bias has yet to be realized. In the 2008 presidential election, polls conducted only by landline were as accurate, in the aggregate, as those that included cell phones.[15] This fortunate outcome reflects a continuation of a pattern documented for several years, whereby the postsurvey demographic weighting, typically used to correct for the over- or underrepresentation of certain groups, also corrects for the bias caused by the missing cell-only respondents.[16] The effectiveness of this correction depends on the assumption that landline and cell-only respondents who share key demographic characteristics (such as being young or Latino) are also similar politically. This assumption remains mostly correct, but evidence emerged in the 2008 election that it is less true than in the past.

In particular, a comparison of landline-accessible and cell-only voters in the exit poll found significant political differences among those age 30 and older (who are, despite the focus on young people, the majority of the cell-only population), suggesting that weighting by age might not eliminate a possible bias. And indeed, preelection telephone surveys conducted by the Pew Research Center confirmed that a small but statistically significant difference in vote preference existed between fully weighted landline samples and combined samples that also included cell phones (Table 2.2).

To demonstrate this, all of Pew's fall preelection polls were combined,

Table 2.2.

Obama Advantage by Type of Telephone Sample

	Landline and cell phone sample	Landline and cell-phone-only sample	Landline sample
Registered voters			
Obama	49.9%	49.4%	48.5%
McCain	40.0%	40.3%	40.9%
Other/Don't know	10.1%	10.3%	10.6%
Obama advantage	+9.9	+9.1	+7.6
Sample size	11,964	10,009	9,229
Likely voters			
Obama	49.8%	49.2%	48.5%
McCain	41.6%	42.1%	42.7%
Other/Don't know	8.6%	8.7%	8.8%
Obama advantage	+8.2	+7.1	+5.8
Sample size	10,919	8,767	8,143

Note: Figures based on weighted data from Pew Research Center preelection polls conducted from September through November 2009 and include those who "lean" toward a candidate.

with a total sample size of nearly 12,000 voters. Three weighted samples were created: (1) the landline sample was weighted as if that had been the only sample available; (2) the landline sample and cell-only voters were combined and weighted; (3) the landline and all cell phone voters were combined and weighted. Barack Obama's lead was slightly—though significantly—higher in the weighted samples that included cell phones. Among likely voters, Obama led by 8.2 percentage points in the combined landline and cell sample, by 7.1 points in the landline and cell-only sample, and by 5.8 points in the landline sample alone. This small difference was not evident in every survey, but it did appear in four of the six. The small size of the apparent bias would not have led to an incorrect forecast in this election, given Obama's final winning margin. But in a closer election it could have mattered. And there is ample evidence from the trends that the potential for bias will continue to grow over the next few years.

Figure 2.2. Young Adults Vanishing from Landline Samples

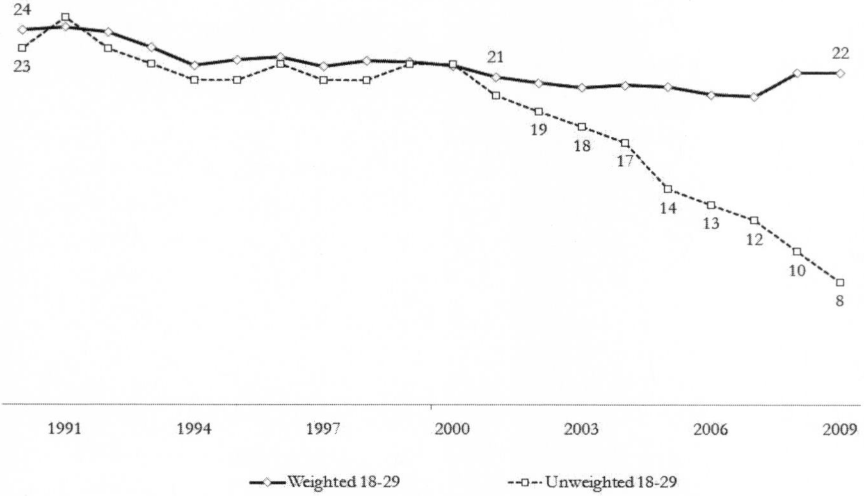

—◇— Weighted 18-29   --□-- Unweighted 18-29

The cell phone challenge may not be limited to cell phone users who have no landline phone. There may also be a potential bias from "cell-mostly" users who have a landline but rarely, if ever, use it. According to the latest report from the National Health Interview Survey, 15.4 percent of adults live in households classified as "wireless mostly."[17] Pew Research's election analysis suggests that the cell-mostly may share some political characteristics with the cell-only, but thus far there is little systematic evidence that landline surveys significantly underrepresent the cell-mostly.

The most serious consequence of noncoverage is bias in survey estimates, but it is not the only negative aspect. Even if weighting can correct for the absence of certain kinds of respondents, they are still missing from the data and unavailable for analysis. This has implications for the depth of analysis that can be done among subgroups and for the precision of estimates based upon those groups.

The problem is particularly acute with respect to the group most likely to be missed by landline surveys: young adults. Beginning in 2002—around the time that government researchers began to note the growth in the cell-only population—the percentage of young adults ages 18–29 in landline samples began to fall. Before that, young people were represented in landline samples at about their proper proportion in the population. Whereas people in this age group constitute slightly more than one in five U.S. adults, Pew's landline samples in 2009 include an average of only 8 percent. In practical terms, this means that a survey of 1,000 respondents should include a little more than 200 young adults, with a margin of error for this group of approximately plus or minus 8 percentage points. However, the typical landline sample will now have only about 80 cases, with a margin of error of 12 points.

Measurement and Other Issues

Other chapters in this volume address the broader question of how well polls reflect what voters really want in an election. But in addition to the mostly political questions inherent in such an inquiry, there are methodological challenges. Two, in particular, faced pollsters in the 2008 presidential election. One is how well surveys capture public attitudes about sensitive issues on which citizens may have reasons to hide or distort their opinions from an interviewer. The second is how well surveys can capture the intensity of opinion and the degree of political engagement among segments of the public. Both were especially salient in 2008.

The presidential contest pitted a young African American candidate with a nontraditional background against an older white candidate who was a war hero from a distinguished military family. How important would race be in the vote? Given the nation's difficult history with race, would voters answer honestly when asked how they were going to vote?

Problems with preelection polls in several high-profile biracial elections in the 1980s and early 1990s suggested that covert racism remained an impediment to black candidates and to accurate polling estimates. White candidates in most of these elections generally did better on Election Day than they were doing in the polls, while their black opponents tended to end up with about the same level of support as the polls indicated they had. This phenomenon was often called the "Bradley effect" because the first claims of its existence occurred in the 1982 race for governor of California. Los Angeles mayor

Tom Bradley, a black Democrat, narrowly lost to Republican George Deukmejian, despite polls showing him with a lead ranging from 9 to 22 points. Although the claim in this instance was controversial, the label stuck.[18]

Among others, three highly visible races in 1989 and 1990 also followed this pattern, though in two instances at least one late poll signaled a closer race. Virginia Democrat and African American Douglas Wilder edged white Republican Marshall Coleman by less than 1 percentage point to become the nation's first elected black governor. But two of three polls conducted just days before the election showed Wilder leading by double digits; a third poll had him 4 points ahead. A similar pattern appeared in the New York City mayoral race the same day and again the following year in a bitter race for the U.S. Senate between African American Democrat Harvey Gantt and Republican incumbent Jesse Helms of North Carolina. Two of three independent polls conducted just before the election showed Gantt leading Helms, but Helms prevailed by 6 percentage points on Election Day.

There were few high-profile elections involving black and white candidates over the next several years. But in 2006 there were five such statewide races for which nonpartisan statewide polling was conducted. In none of the five did any clear sign of bias appear. The most relevant test case appeared to be the contest for the U.S. Senate in Tennessee, which matched black Democrat Harold Ford Jr. and white Republican Bob Corker. Ford narrowly lost to Corker, 51 percent to 48 percent. Many preelection polls were conducted for this race, and two of the final four polls actually overstated Corker's lead.

These and other polls provided some assurance that the Bradley effect might be a thing of the past.[19] But in the very first primary of the 2008 Democratic nomination season, the polls experienced a spectacular failure that raised the concerns anew. Despite leading in the polls by an average of 8 points, Barack Obama lost the New Hampshire primary to Hillary Clinton by 3 points. Every major poll—approximately twelve in all—called the election wrong. A subsequent investigation by an expert panel convened by the American Association for Public Opinion Research failed to identify a clear reason for the polls' failure, but racial bias did not appear to be a factor.[20] This point was amplified by the fact that a similar bias failed to appear in the following primaries, which took place across a wide range of states and

Table 2.3.

Race-of-Interviewer Effect on Candidate Support among Registered
White Non-Hispanic Voters

	White Non-Hispanic interviewer (%)		Black Non-Hispanic interviewer (%)	
	Obama	McCain	Obama	McCain
All white voters				
Mid-September	38	53	36	52
Late September	40	49	41	48
Early October	40	52	44	47
Mid-October	42	48	47	43
Late October	41	42	43	48
Election weekend	44	46	42	46
White Democrats and Democratic-Leaning Independents				
Mid-September	87	8	79	10
Late September	84	10	91	6
Early October	91	4	87	8
Mid-October	88	6	91	4
Late October	82	6	89	7
Election weekend	88	6	85	7

Note: Percentages based on weighted data from Pew Research Center preelection polls conducted from September through November 2008.

political cultures. In fact, the most consistent observation about subsequent primary polling in the Democratic race was that Obama's support was underestimated more frequently than it was overestimated.

Still, interest in the possibility of a Bradley effect remained high, and pollsters were asked repeatedly about the issue throughout the fall campaign season. The accuracy of the final polls, at both the national and the state levels, indicates that voters generally did what they told pollsters they were going to do. But pollsters were concerned, and many took steps to gauge potential hidden racial bias.

It has long been observed that respondents sometimes give different answers to racially sensitive questions depending on whether the interviewer is black or white; one such example was seen in the Virginia gubernatorial race in 1989, an election that seemed to reflect a Bradley effect.[21] In 2008, the Pew Research Center conducted ongoing analyses of possible race-of-interviewer effects in its fall polls. As Table 2.3 shows, there was no evidence of a race-of-interviewer effect. The only poll in which a significant difference appeared showed an effect in the "wrong" direction, with more white Democrats telling white interviewers than black interviewers that they intended to vote for Obama. A multivariate analysis confirmed the null finding.[22]

None of this is to say that race was not a factor in the election; undoubtedly it was, given the current political alignments in the United States: most African Americans identify with the Democratic Party or lean Democratic, while the GOP's adherents are mostly white.[23] But the issue for polling is whether the public accurately reports its beliefs and intentions to pollsters, and in this election, at least, evidently it did.

Voter Intensity and Early Voting

The 2008 election was held at the end of the presidency of one of the most polarizing political figures of modern times, and the electorate—especially on the Democratic side—was highly energized. Among the strongest supporters of Obama were young people, who historically turn out at levels far below those of older voters. Would young people really show up? And at least some evidence from the primaries suggested that pollsters had underestimated the turnout of African American voters. Would this be a problem in the general election? Finally, all signs pointed to the possibility that a record number of people would vote before Election Day, aided by election laws facilitating early voting and organizing campaigns urging people to avoid the possibility of long lines and other problems on November 4.

The evidence indicates that pollsters did a good job gauging the intensity and the intentions of voters. National polling organizations offering forecasts that about one-third of voters would cast a ballot before Election Day were generally correct. Similarly, most built assumptions regarding somewhat higher African American and youth turnout into their models. Overall turnout did not rise as much as some observers had forecast. According to George Mason University's Michael McDonald, a national authority on voter turnout, the percentage of the voting-eligible population that turned out was 62.3 percent, up from 60.7 percent.

The Consequences
Cost-Related Changes in the Landscape

Thus far, political polling has met the challenges. But the price has been considerable. Growing nonresponse means that greater effort is needed to obtain a sample of a given size, and even greater effort is needed if the goal is to limit the decline in response rates that would otherwise occur. The coverage issue is even more serious. Adding cell phone interviews to a poll is very expensive. In Pew Research's experience, the cost of a cell phone interview is approximately twice that of a landline interview. If the design calls for screening to reach cell-only adults, the cost per interview is approximately four times as much. The costs result from several factors: calls must be dialed manually (rather than by machine) because of telecommunications law designed to protect cell phone owners from having to pay for unwanted calls; a high percentage of cell phone numbers are answered by minors—between one-third and 40 percent in Pew's experience—and are thus ineligible for inclusion in the survey; the payment of reimbursements to cell phone respondents for the costs they might incur in taking the call (not all survey organizations offer these); and the higher administrative and technical costs incurred in adding an additional sample.[24]

Collectively, these additional costs have led many media organizations—which are facing financial problems from many sources—to cut back or abandon polling altogether. News editors have described polling as a "commodity" that does not justify the handcrafted prices it seems to command. Among the high-profile newspaper polls that have gone out of business in the past couple of years are the Los Angeles Times Poll, one of the pioneers among the media polling community, and the *Minneapolis Star Tribune*'s poll. The loss of this type of polling expertise from news organizations is felt not only in the fact that they are no longer producing their own polling but also in the absence of staff expertise that can help inform the organization's coverage of other polling. News organizations like ABC News or the *Washington Post* depend on their resident polling experts to review and vet survey research conducted by others before it can appear on the air or in the newspaper.

Interactive Voice Response Polls

Many national polls of good quality remain, but even they are squeezed financially. State and local polls are more seriously affected, both because news organizations and universities—two important funders—are under serious financial pressure and because state and local polling organizations face nearly insurmountable obstacles to including cell phones in their samples. One response has been the rapid growth of interactive voice response (IVR), usually referred to as robo-polls. These polls are typically conducted on landline samples (since federal law prohibits dialing cell phone samples with these devices). But they can also be used on voter registration files. Automatic dialing machines call the numbers; when the phone is answered, a recorded voice—sometimes a local television anchor—provides a brief introduction and then asks a few questions, which the respondent can answer by pressing keys on the phone or saying the appropriate number or word.

These polls seemingly violate many elements of the survey canon's best practices—they have only a rudimentary ability to select a respondent within a household, no live interviewer to establish a rapport with respondents, little assurance that respondents are actually adults and eligible to participate, no ability to provide answers to questions about the purpose of the study or who is sponsoring. Despite these limitations, IVR polling has compiled an impressive record of accuracy in election forecasting. In 2008, IVR polls in state-level presidential election contests had a candidate error rate of 1.5 percent, compared with an error rate of 1.6 percent for polls with live interviewers.[25]

IVR polls have very low response rates—often well below 10 percent—but illustrate why it's possible that other polling continues to accurately represent the population despite precipitous declines in response rates. They suggest that the propensity to respond to polls varies by time and circumstance—people are busy, unavailable, tired, or otherwise unamenable, but not always. The likelihood of answering such a call and cooperating for a short survey is evidently only weakly correlated with opinions on the substantive topics in the poll. To the extent that this is true for longer polls with live interviewers, declining response rates have not undercut their accuracy. The paradigm underlying this theory is that the propensity to respond to a survey is stochastic. That is, people cannot be divided into two classes—those amenable to participating and those who won't do so. Instead, nearly everyone has a variable likelihood of taking part, and a person's propensity to do so is a function of many factors, some but not all related to the content of the survey.

The Achilles heel of IVR surveys is not their response rate but the fact that they do not include cell phones and cannot as long as they rely on automatic dialing machines. Jay Leve, president of SurveyUSA, a prominent IVR firm, has said that his per-interview costs are one-fourth of those of live interviewer surveys but that including cell phones would change this to one-half—still an advantage but perhaps not enough to remain financially viable. Thus, as response rates decline and noncoverage grows, IVR may not be able to keep up. Leve said as much in his presentation at the Joint Statistical Meetings in August 2009, observing that his business, as well as that of conventional telephone survey researchers, was likely in its final years.[26]

IVR polling has one other serious liability that limits its value: IVR polls must be relatively brief, which means they are ill suited to policy-related surveys that require in-depth questioning on a subject. Despite their accuracy in election forecasting, they are rarely used by political professionals to conduct the broad polling that helps candidates understand the nature of the electorate they face, the variety of issues of importance to voters, or the types of messages most likely to resonate with voters in targeted groups. Similarly, IVR polls are typically not employed by news organizations that need to probe public attitudes about complex issues in detail.

The Fixes

Once landline telephone penetration reached a critical threshold in the 1970s, surveyors began shifting their work away from personal interviews, accepting some of the limitations that the new mode imposed on them (the inability to use "show cards" or to conduct very lengthy interviews) and taking advantage of opportunities opened by the new mode (the chance to personally supervise all or most of the interviews or the ability to conduct a large number of interviews in a very short period of time).

As it did with challenges in the past, the survey research profession has responded to its current problems with the introduction of new methods to offset the limitations of approaches that are becoming obsolete or impractical, as well as greater effort using its current tools. In the former category are dual-frame telephone surveys, discussed in brief earlier; surveys using the Internet; and mixed-mode surveys. For many research goals there is an increasing reliance on nonsurvey approaches that utilize large databases of consumer and political information about households and individuals. These will be discussed briefly in the last section of this chapter.

Dual-Frame Surveys

Many pollsters have responded to the coverage problem created by the cell phone by adding cell phone samples to their studies. Many screen cell phone respondents for the cell-phone-only group, while others, including the Pew Research Center, interview all adults reached in their cell phone samples. Either approach solves the coverage issue, and the method that interviews all adults reached by cell phone also addresses the issue of the cell-phone-mostly population, should this group pose a risk of bias to landline plus cell-only samples. Because many households that formerly could not afford telephone service—due to the high monthly bills, connection charges, or credit history required—can now afford at least a "disposable" cell phone, more of the population is reachable by phone than in the heyday of the landline.

Many of the concerns about including cell phones have not proven to be a problem. There is no indication that the quality of data gathered on cell phones is inferior to that obtained by landline.[27] There is also little indication that interviews by cell phone need to be shorter than those on landline. And while survey organizations' experiences vary, cell phone response rates do not appear to be consistently worse than landline response rates. In Pew Research's experience, there has been no difference at all.

But many problems do exist. Perhaps the most significant is cost, as noted earlier. Another is the difficulty of combining cell phone and landline samples. Landline surveys typically randomly select one adult from a household to be interviewed, whereas most cell phone surveys interview the person who answers the phone, on the assumption that the cell phone is a personal device. This assumption is not always valid, but even when it is, the blending of landline and cell samples is tricky. There is also the problem of adequate parameters for weighting. Census surveys provide rock-solid demographic parameters for overall targets in survey weighting, but the only large government survey available that provides demographic information about the population by telephone usage is the National Health Interview Survey, which interviews fewer than 13,000 households for its semiannual estimates. Although these data are irreplaceable for the survey community, they do not permit estimates on small subgroups or many individual states.

Sampling cell phones is also much less precise than sampling landlines. Although most landline samples are random digit dial, giving nearly every landline number a known chance of inclusion in the sample, their efficiency for use in surveys is greatly enhanced by the use of directory listings. This is not possible for cell phone samples. More important, the geographic information—so important for subnational survey work with landlines—is far less accurate for cell phones.[28]

All these problems have made dual-frame surveys a less-than-optimal response to the coverage problem. But the situation is improving as survey firms gain more experience with cell phone samples and clients realize that without cell phone samples certain important subgroups such as young people will simply be out of reach. Moreover, dual-frame surveys have the credibility that the profession needs as users of survey data realize the limitations of the landline telephone survey.

Internet Polling

Nearly eight in ten adults (79 percent) use the Internet, according to the Pew Internet & American Life Project. The rate of growth in Internet adoption has slowed in the past four years but continues to inch up. Given the broad adoption of the Net, the essentially costless nature of an "interview" conducted on the Web, and the Internet's potential for allowing the presentation of text, videos, and other visual material in interviews, it is no surprise that it has become the mode of choice for much survey research. There is no widely accepted estimate of how many surveys are conducted on the Internet or what share of all political polling is done there, but ABC polling director Gary Langer reported that nearly half of all market research spending this year will be for online data.[29]

There is little debate that the Internet as a survey mode has numerous advantages over in-person interviews or the telephone. Even some of its liabilities carry a methodological silver lining. For example, the absence of a live interviewer means that questions cannot be clarified for respondents or obvious misinterpretations by the respondents corrected. But on the plus side, an Internet interview may be less subject to social desirability bias and so-called interviewer effects that result from differences between interviewers. Systematic comparisons of telephone and Internet interviews have found that the Internet may be better with regard to some dimensions of data quality.[30]

The big problem for Internet surveys is sampling. There is no feasible way to randomly sample Internet users using the Internet. No directory of e-mail addresses exists, and even if it did, the blizzard of legitimate messages—not to mention spam—received by the average user would relegate a survey invitation from an unknown source to a very low priority for response. The Internet is an excellent mode for data collection from populations where a list exists and a preexisting relationship between the survey sponsor and the list exists. But without these very difficult preconditions, sampling from the Internet in a way analogous to telephone sampling is impossible.

A more scientifically feasible but somewhat expensive Internet sampling model was developed by the company Knowledge Networks, founded by political scientists Douglas Rivers and Norman Nie. A random sample of households was recruited by telephone (and now telephone and mail) and invited to join a large panel of respondents, who participate in a minimum number of surveys in exchange for modest incentives. Households without Internet service were provided with Web access. Knowledge Networks has conducted numerous political surveys since its inception in 1998, including much of the data collection for the 2008 National Election Study and frequent surveys for CBS News. A small number of similar panels have existed, but this model has not yet found widespread adoption because of the comparatively high costs and technical challenges in maintaining an ongoing survey panel. And even Knowledge Networks faces the same problems of relatively low total response rates that plague other surveys, as well as problems unique to panels, such as attrition and panel conditioning.

The limitations on sampling have not stopped numerous organizations from establishing Internet samples based on convenience samples of people recruited on the Internet to take part in online surveys. Many, if not most, of the major marketing research companies maintain or use such panels for at least some of their work. The reason is simple: Internet panels are far cheaper than telephone surveys of random samples. But there is a lot of concern about data quality.[31] In 2006, a research executive for Procter & Gamble told an industry forum that the quality of the market research data the company was getting from online panels had been deteriorating and that it was increasingly hard to trust the data. That discussion led to a major effort to establish higher standards for online panels, though not to a reconsideration of the decision to use nonprobability methods. The results of this effort to improve data quality are inconclusive. Because of the inability to generalize from online nonprobability samples to the general public with a known degree of accuracy, organizations such as Pew Research do not use such methods for polling intended to represent the general public, and they are not commonly employed by political pollsters in campaigns for the same reasons. Only three organizations conducted public preelection polls in 2008 using Internet samples, according to an analysis by the National Council for Public Polls.[32] The experience of one—YouGov/Polimetrix, which conducted the vast majority of the polls in that election—offers hope that the Internet may yet be harnessed for good-quality political research.

YouGov/Polimetrix was founded in 2004 by one of the creators of Knowledge Networks, Douglas Rivers. While its underlying panel of respondents is recruited using methods similar to those for other Internet panels, the construction of its samples for individual polling and analysis is quite different. Individuals from its panel are matched to a probability sample of adults on a number of characteristics including demographics and political attitudes. The method is analogous to case-control studies in epidemiology, an accepted—although nonprobability—methodology in the medical research field. YouGov/Polimetrix's track record in election forecasts is good.

Of course, critics charge that the *Literary Digest*'s large mail-in presidential election poll early in the twentieth century was accurate, too—until it wasn't. Despite having millions of respondents in the 1936 election, the poll incorrectly forecast that Alf Landon would defeat Franklin Roosevelt. The fear is that a good track record for a nonprobability method is not a reliable guide to changed circumstances in the future, such as an electorate realigned around a different set of issues.[33]

Mixed-Mode Surveys and Address-Based Sampling

One other solution to the current problems facing polling assumes that the public today is diverse and communicates with the world in a variety of ways. Accordingly, the way to ensure greater coverage and higher response rates is to use multiple methods of approach and offer more than one way for people to participate in an interview. Multimode surveys are nothing new in the survey field, but they are rarely used in political polling. That may be changing. Many panel surveys entail recruitment by one mode and response by another, or by more than one mode. Multimode surveys make it possible to construct samples from more than one source, helping to reduce coverage error, and then allow respondents to participate using a mode that is most convenient to them.

In particular, researchers are increasingly experimenting with address-based sampling. Pollsters can sample from the U.S. Postal Service's master list of all addresses, which provides coverage of more than 95 percent of all adults. Contact can be made by mail or by telephone (by matching the addresses with information from telephone directory listings and other databases). Address-based sampling is currently employed by the media research organizations Nielsen and Arbitron and has been successfully tested on a variety of health surveys.[34]

One of the most important benefits of address-based sampling is the ability to sample precisely from small geographic areas, a difficult challenge for telephone surveys (especially cell phones). For the numerous political surveys that require information from subnational populations, this method holds considerable promise.

Such studies entail significant challenges in management and coordination, and the statistical issues in combining samples from multiple frames are daunting. But the fragmented and segmented public of 2009—and beyond—may provide pollsters with little choice. Just as there is no longer a majority of the nation gathered around the evening news on just three television networks, there may no longer be a single best way to reach and recruit a voter or citizen to take part in a survey.

The Future

For journalists, scholars, campaign professionals, and candidates, a valid political poll is an essential tool in understanding—and affecting—what happens in elections and in governing. Town hall meetings, constituent mail, and campaign contributions all convey intensity of sentiment and even financial clout. But only representative public opinion polls provide a view of the public in which everyone is equal. In Verba's view, polls offer a corrective to the status bias in American politics—that some citizens are more influential than others because they have more money, more political acumen, and more access.[35]

But polling's problems increasingly undermine its ability to provide this unbiased model of the public. Practicing pollsters are well aware that the craft of survey research is built on a never-ending series of trade-offs. With finite resources, money or effort expended on one aspect of the research is necessarily taken from some other aspect. Addressing growing noncoverage and nonresponse, though vital, forces cutbacks elsewhere—in total sample size, in pretesting, in the length of the instrument, in qualitative work to accompany the survey. Only the pollster, guided by the priorities of the clientele or audience for the research, can decide what the optimal allocation of resources should be. That decision will often be controversial in the eyes of other pollsters.

New modalities, and greater effort and resources devoted to the current modalities, offer potential solutions—or at least more years of viability. In the face of these challenges, researchers are increasingly employing the power of large databases and robust computers to develop insights about political behavior. For some purposes, such as the targeting of messages and mobilization in elections, these methods are undoubtedly effective and here to stay. But their ability to provide the insights we rely upon to make sense of elections, major policy debates, the arrival of new political actors, and other phenomena is unproven. And their ability to ensure representation of all Americans is even less certain, given the data sources for such analyses.

Our faith that polling's problems will find a solution rests less with any particular technological innovation, mathematical method, or new database than with the conviction that human beings remain interested in the world around them and fundamentally amenable to offering their perspective and reactions to strangers who ask, despite the myriad distractions of the world and the suspicions and concerns that many of us have about inquiries from strangers. That is one of the lessons of survey research's continued viability in the face of precipitous declines in response rates. People are harder to reach and persuade to cooperate, but polls need to understand that "it's nothing personal." As long as people continue to want to use their political voice, under at least some circumstance, the quest to keep polling viable will not fail.

NOTES

1. Sidney Verba, "The Citizen as Respondent: Sample Surveys and American Democracy," *American Political Science Review* 90 (1996): 1–7.

2. Scott Keeter, Jocelyn Kiley, Leah Christian, and Michael Dimock, "Perils of Polling in the 2008 Election" (paper presented at the annual meeting of the American Association for Public Opinion Research, Hollywood, FL, May 14–17, 2009).

3. Mark Blumenthal, "Is Polling As We Know It Doomed?" *National Journal,* August 10, 2009, www.nationaljournal.com/njonline/mp_20090810_1804.php (accessed September 24, 2009).

4. The Current Population Survey makes its initial household contact and interview in person but attempts to conduct interviews in subsequent waves by telephone.

5. Richard Curtin, Stanley Presser, and Eleanor Singer, "Changes in Telephone Survey Nonresponse over the Past Quarter Century," *Public Opinion Quarterly* 69 (2005): 87–98.

6. Allyson Holbrook, Jon Krosnick, and Alison Pfent, "The Causes and Consequences of Response Rates in Surveys by the News Media and Government Contractor Survey Research Firms," in *Advances in Telephone Survey Methodology,* ed. James M. Lepkowski, N. Clyde Tucker, J. Michael Brick, Edith D. De Leeuw, Lilli Japec, Paul J. Lavrakas, Michael W. Link, and Roberta L. Sangster, 499–528 (New York: Wiley, 2007); Curtin, Presser and Singer, "Changes in Telephone Survey Nonresponse."

7. National Council on Public Polls (NCPP), "NCPP Analysis of Final Presidential Pre-Election Polls, 2008," www.ncpp.org/files/NCPP_2008_analysis_of_election_polls_121808%20 pdf_0.pdf (accessed September 24, 2009).

8. Scott Keeter, Carolyn Miller, Andrew Kohut, Robert M. Groves, and Stanley Presser, "Consequences of Reducing Nonresponse in a National Telephone Survey," *Public Opinion*

Quarterly 64 (2000): 125–48; Scott Keeter, Courtney Kennedy, Michael Dimock, Jonathan Best, and Peyton Craighill, "Gauging the Impact of Growing Nonresponse on Estimates from a National RDD Telephone Survey," *Public Opinion Quarterly* 70 (2006): 759–79.

9. Richard Curtin, Stanley Presser, and Eleanor Singer, "The Effects of Response Rate Changes on the Index of Consumer Sentiment," *Public Opinion Quarterly* 64 (2000): 413–28.

10. "Primary Problems: How Exit Pollsters Prepare to Cope with the Super-Crowded Election Season," Pew Research Center Publications, September 14, 2007, www.pewresearch.org/pubs/662/exit-polls-primary-problems (accessed April 10, 2010).

11. Katharine G. Abraham, Aaron Maitland, and Suzanne M. Bianchi, "Nonresponse in the American Time Use Survey: Who Is Missing from the Data and How Much Does It Matter?" *Public Opinion Quarterly* 70 (2006): 676–703.

12. Stephen J. Blumberg and Julian V. Luke, "Wireless Substitution: Early Release of Estimates from the National Health Interview Survey, July–December 2009," *National Center for Health Statistics,* May 2010, www.cdc.gov/nchs/data/nhis/earlyrelease/wireless201005.htm (accessed July 25, 2010); Owen T. Thornberry and James T. Massey, "Trends in United States Telephone Coverage across Time and Subgroups," in *Telephone Survey Methodology.* ed. Robert M. Groves, Paul P. Biemer, Lars E. Lyberg, James T. Massey, William L. Nicholls II, and Joseph Waksberg, 25–50 (New York: Wiley, 1988).

13. Blumberg and Luke, "Wireless Substitution."

14. These included ABC/*Washington Post,* CBS/*New York Times,* Gallup, Ipsos/McClatchy, NBC/*Wall St. Journal,* and the Pew Research Center.

15. Scott Keeter, Michael Dimock, and Leah Christian, "Calling Cell Phones in '08 Pre-Election Polls," Pew Research Center for the People & the Press, December 18, 2008, www.people-press.org/reports/pdf/cell-phone-commentary.pdf (accessed May 22, 2009); Gary Langer, Peyton Craighill, Patrick Moynihan, Jon Cohen, Jennifer Agiesta, and Dave Lambert, "'These Nutty Pollsters': Methodological Issues in ABC News/Washington Post 2008 Pre-Election Polling" (paper presented at the annual meeting of the American Association for Public Opinion Research, Hollywood, FL, May 14–17, 2009).

16. Scott Keeter, Courtney Kennedy, April Clark, Trevor Tompson, and Mike Mokrzycki, "What's Missing from National Landline RDD Surveys? The Impact of the Growing Cell-Only Population," *Public Opinion Quarterly* 71 (2007): 772–92.

17. Blumberg and Luke, "Wireless Substitution."

18. Among others, Republican pollster Lance Tarrance has questioned whether there was a Bradley effect in 1982. His reminder of this skepticism appeared in 2008; see Lance Tarrance, "The Bradly Effect—Selective Memory," *Real Clear Politics,* www.realclearpolitics.com/articles/2008/10/the_bradley_effect_selective_m.html (accessed April 14, 2010).

19. Daniel J. Hopkins, "No More Wilder Effect, Never a Whitman Effect: When and Why Polls Mislead about Black and Female Candidates," *Journal of Politics* (in press); manuscript (2008) available at www.people.iq.harvard.edu/~dhopkins/wilder13.pdf (accessed May 27, 2009).

20. American Association for Public Opinion Research (AAPOR), "An Evaluation of the Methodology of the 2008 Pre-Election Primary Polls," www.aapor.org/uploads/AAPOR_Press_Releases/AAPOR_Rept_of_the_ad_hoc_committee.pdf (accessed May 12, 2009).

21. Thomas M. Guterbock, Steven E. Finkel, and Marian J. Borg, "Race of Interviewer Effects in a Pre Election Poll," *Public Opinion Quarterly* 55 (1991): 313–30.

22. Keeter et al., "Consequences of Reducing Nonresponse in a National Telephone Survey."

23. Two studies of the 2008 election go further in arguing that race was a key factor in voting decisions; see Vincent L. Hutchings, "Change or More of the Same? Evaluating Racial Attitudes in the Obama Era," *Public Opinion Quarterly* 73 (2009): 917–42; Josh Pasek, Alexander Tahk, Yphtach Lelkes, Jon A. Krosnick, B. Keith Payne, Omair Akhtar, and Trevor Tompson, "Determinants of Turnout and Candidate Choice in the 2008 U.S. Presidential Election: Illuminating the Impact of Racial Prejudice and Other Considerations," *Public Opinion Quarterly* 73 (2009): 943–94.

24. Federal law continues to protect cell phone owners from automatic-dialed solicitations, www.fcc.gov/cgb/consumerfacts/tcpa.html (accessed April 14, 2010).

25. These data are from the National Council of Public Polls (NCPP), which defines candidate error as one-half of the difference between the actual margin of victory in the election and the poll's predicted margin of victory.

26. Blumenthal, "Is Polling As We Know It Doomed?"

27. Courtney Kennedy, Stephen E. Everett, and Michael W. Traugott, "Use of Cognitive Shortcuts in Landline and Cell Phone Surveys" (paper presented at the annual meeting of the American Association for Public Opinion Research, Hollywood, FL, May 14–17, 2009); AAPOR, "Evaluation of the Methodology of the 2008 Pre-Election Primary Polls."

28. Leah M. Christian, Michael Dimock, and Scott Keeter, "Accurately Locating Where Wireless Respondents Live Requires More Than a Phone Number" (paper presented at the annual meeting of the American Association for Public Opinion Research, Hollywood, FL, May 14–17, 2009); available at www.pewresearch.org/pubs/1278/cell-phones-geographic-sampling-problems (accessed September 1, 2009).

29. Gary Langer, "Study Finds Trouble for Opt-in Internet Surveys," *The Numbers,* September 1, 2009, www.blogs.abcnews.com/thenumbers/2009/09/study-finds-trouble-for-internet-surveys.html (accessed September 24, 2009).

30. LinChiat Chang and Jon A. Krosnick, "National Surveys via RDD Telephone Interviewing vs. the Internet: Comparing Sample Representativeness and Response Quality," *Public Opinion Quarterly* (in press).

31. Ibid.

32. NCPP, "NCPP Analysis of Final Presidential Pre-Election Polls, 2008."

33. Peverill Squire, "Why the 1936 Literary Digest Poll Failed," *Public Opinion Quarterly* 52 (1988):125–33.

34. Susan Sherr, David Dutwin, Timothy Triplett, Doug Wissoker, and Sharon Long, "Comparing Random Digit Dial (RDD) and United States Postal Service (USPS) Address-Based Sample Designs for a General Population Survey: The 2008 Massachusetts Health Insurance Survey" (paper presented at the annual meeting of the American Association for Public Opinion Research, Hollywood, FL, May 14–17, 2009).

35. Verba, "Citizen as Respondent."

3

Can I Trust This Poll?

MARK BLUMENTHAL

What makes a public opinion poll "scientific?" If you had asked that question of a random sample of pollsters twenty-three years ago when I started my first job at a polling firm, you would have heard far more agreement than today. Now, many more pollsters are asking fundamental questions about the best practices of our profession, and their growing uncertainty makes it ever harder to answer the question I hear most often from readers of Pollster. com: "Can I trust this poll?"

Let's take a step back and consider the elements that most pollsters deem essential to obtaining a high-quality, representative survey. The fundamental principle behind the term "scientific" is the random probability sample. The idea is to draw a sample in a way that every member of the population of interest has an equal probability of being selected (or at least, to be a little technical, a probability that is both known and greater than zero). As long as the process of selection and response is truly random and unbiased, a sample of a thousand or a few hundred will be representative within a predictable range of variation, popularly known as the "margin of error."

Pollsters disagreed with each other, even twenty or thirty years ago, about the practical steps necessary to obtain a random sample of Americans. However, at the dawn of my career, at a time when more than 90 percent of American households had landline telephone service, pollsters were much closer to consensus than they are now on the steps necessary to draw a representative sample by telephone. These included:

- A true random sample of known working telephone numbers produced by a method known as random digit dial (RDD) that randomly generates the final digits in order to reach both listed and unlisted phones.
- Coverage of the population in excess of 90 percent, possible by telephone only with RDD sampling (in the pre–cell phone era) but almost never (decades ago) through official lists of registered voters.
- Persistence in efforts to reach selected households. Pollsters would call *at least* three or four different times on *at least* three or four successive evenings in order to get those who might be out of the house on the first or second call.
- A "reasonable" response rate (although pollsters differed, then as now, about the meaning of "reasonable").
- Random selection of an individual within each selected household, or at least a method closer to random than just interviewing the first person to answer the phone, something that usually skews the sample toward older women.
- The use of live interviewers—preferred for a variety of reasons, but among the most important was the presumed need for a human touch to gain respondent cooperation.
- Weighting (or statistically adjusting) to correct any small bias in the demographic representation (gender, age, race, etc.) as compared with estimates produced by the U.S. Census, but *never* weighting by theoretically changeable attitudes like party identification.

I am probably guilty of oversimplifying. Pollsters have always disagreed about the specifics of some of these practices, and they have always adopted different standards. Still, from my perspective, these characteristics are the hallmarks of quality sampling for many of my colleagues—especially those I see every year at the conferences of the American Association for Public Opinion Research (AAPOR).[1]

The application of these principles has shifted slightly in recent years, even among traditionalists, in two ways: First, pollsters are no longer convinced that a low response rate is inherently problematic. In fact, they have learned that some efforts to boost response rates can actually make results less accurate.[2] Second, to combat the rapid declines in coverage posed by cell-phone-only households, many national media pollsters now also interview Americans on their mobile phones, using supplemental samples of cell phone numbers to boost sample coverage back above 90 percent. But by and large, traditional pollsters still use the same standards to define the makings of a "scientific" survey as they did twenty or thirty years ago.

A new breed of pollsters has come to the fore, however, that routinely breaks some or all of these rules. None exemplifies the trend better than Scott Rasmussen and the surveys he publishes at RasmussenReports.com. Here I want to be clear: I single out Rasmussen Reports in this chapter not to condemn Rasmussen's methods but to make a point about the current state of "best practices" in the polling profession, especially as perceived by those who follow and depend on survey data.

Rasmussen's sampling and calling procedures are consistent with the framework I describe in only one respect: they use a form of random digit dial sampling to select telephone numbers (although Rasmussen's methodology page says only that "calls are placed to randomly-selected phone numbers through a process that ensures appropriate geographic representation").[3] In other ways, however, Rasmussen's methods differ: they use an automated, recorded voice methodology (known as interactive voice response, or IVR) rather than live interviewers. They conduct most surveys in a single evening and never dial a selected number more than once. They routinely weight samples by party identification. They cannot interview respondents on their mobile phones (something legally prohibited when automated methods are used) and thus achieve a coverage rate well below 90 percent.

If you had described Rasmussen's methods to me at the dawn of my career, I probably would have dismissed them the way my friend Michael Traugott, a University of Michigan professor and former AAPOR president, did nine years ago. "Until there is more information about their methods and a longer track record to evaluate their results," he wrote, "we shouldn't confuse the work they do with scientific surveys, and it shouldn't be called polling."[4]

But that was then. In 2008 and 2009, Traugott chaired an AAPOR committee that looked into the preelection polling problems in New Hampshire and other presidential primary states in 2008. The committee's report concluded that use of "interactive voice response (IVR) techniques made no difference to the accuracy of estimates" in the primary polls. In other words, automated surveys, including Rasmussen's, were "about equally accurate" in the states they examined.[5]

Consider also the analysis of Nate Silver. On his Web site FiveThirtyEight. com last year, he approached the issue of survey quality from the perspective of the accuracy of polls in predicting election outcomes rather than their underlying methodology. He gathered past polling data from 171 contests for president, governor, and U.S. Senate fielded since 2000 and calculated accuracy scores for each pollster. His study rated Rasmussen as the third most accurate of thirty-two pollsters, just behind SurveyUSA, another automated pollster.[6] When Silver compared eight daily polls tracking the presidential contest last fall, Rasmussen ranked first. He concluded that Rasmussen, "with its large sample size and high pollster rating—would probably be the one I'd want with me on a desert island."[7]

The point here is not to praise or condemn any particular approach to polling but to highlight the serious issues now confronting the profession. Put simply, at a time when pollsters are finding it harder to reach and interview representative samples, the consumers of polling data do not perceive "quality" the same way that pollsters do. Moreover, the success of automated surveys in estimating election "horse race" results, and the ongoing transition in communications technology, have left many pollsters struggling to agree on best practices and questioning the some of the profession's long-accepted orthodoxies.

The question for the rest of us, in this period of transition, remains the same: How do we know which polls to trust? Those who assess polls and pollsters generally fall into two categories: those who check the methodology and those who check the results. Let's consider both.

Check the Methods

Most pollsters have been trained to assess polls by looking at their underlying methods, not the results they produce. The idea is that you do all you can to contact and interview a truly random sample, ask standardized, balanced, clearly worded questions, and then trust the results. Four years ago, my colleagues at *The Hotline* asked pollsters how they determine whether they have a good sample. The answer from Gary Langer, director of polling at ABC News, best captures this philosophy:

A good sample is determined not by what comes out of a survey but what goes into it: Rigorous methodology including carefully designed probability sampling, field work and tabulation procedures. If you've started worrying about a "good sample" at the end of the process, it's probably too late for you to have one.[8]

A big practical challenge in applying this philosophy is that the definition of "rigorous methodology" can get very subjective. While many pollsters agree on general principles (as described above), we lack consensus on a specific set of best practices. Pollsters disagree, for example, about the best process used to choose a respondent in sampled households. They disagree about how many times to dial before giving up on a phone number or about the ideal length of time a poll should be in the field. They disagree about when it's appropriate to sample from a list of registered voters, about which weighting procedures are most appropriate, about whether automated interviewing methods are acceptable, and more.

This lack of consensus has several sources: the need to adapt methods to unique situations, differing assessments of the trade-offs between various potential sources of error, and the usual tensions between the goals of cost and quality. Yet whatever the reason, these varying subjective judgments make it all but impossible to score poll quality using a set of objective criteria. All too often, methodological quality is in the eye of the beholder.

A bigger problem is that the underlying assumption—that these rigorous, random digit methods produce truly random probability samples—is weakening. The *unweighted* samples obtained by national pollsters now routinely underrepresent younger and nonwhite adults while routinely overrepresenting white and college-educated Americans. Of course, virtually all pollsters weight their completed samples demographically to correct these skews. Also, many pollsters are now using supplemental samples to interview Americans on their cell phones in order to improve coverage of the younger cell-phone-only population.

Most of the time, this approach seems to work. Preelection polls continued to perform well during the 2008 general election, matching or exceeding their performance in 2004 and prior years.[9] But how long will it be before the assumptions of what SurveyUSA's Jay Leve calls "barge in polling" give way to a world in which most Americans treat a ringing phone from an unknown number the way they treat unsolicited spam e-mail?[10] And when it does, how will we evaluate the newer forms of research?

Check the Results

When nonpollsters think about how to evaluate polls, their intuition points in a different direction. They will ask, simply, how accurate is the pollster? The popularity of Nate Silver and the pollster ratings he posted at FiveThirtyEight.com in 2008 speaks to the desire of nonpollsters to reduce this issue to one simple accuracy score.[11]

Pollsters, too, understand the importance of the perceived accuracy of their work. "The performance of election polls," wrote Scott Keeter and his Pew Research Center colleagues in 2009, "is no mere trophy for the polling community, for the credibility of the entire survey research profession depends to a great degree on how election polls match the objective standard of election outcomes."[12]

So what's the problem with using accuracy scores to evaluate individual pollsters? Consider some important challenges. First, pollsters do not agree on the best way to score accuracy, with the core disagreement centering on how to treat the undecided percentage that appears nowhere on the ballot. And for good reason. Differences in scoring can often produce very different pollster accuracy rankings.[13]

Second, the usual random variation in individual poll results due to simple sampling error gives especially prolific pollsters—those active in many contests—an advantage in the aggregate scores over those that poll in relatively few contests. Comparisons for individual pollsters get dicey when the number of polls used to compute the score gets low.

Third, and probably most important, scoring accuracy this way tells us about only one particular measure (the vote preference question) on one type of survey (preelection) at one point in the campaign (usually the final week). Consider Figure 3.1 (prepared by my colleague Charles Franklin). It plots the Obama-minus-McCain margin on roughly 350 surveys that tracked national popular vote between June and November 2008. An assessment of pollster error would consider only the final twenty or so surveys—the points plotted in gray.

Notice how the spread of results (and the frequency of outliers) is much

Figure 3.1. Obama Minus McCain Margin, June–November 2008

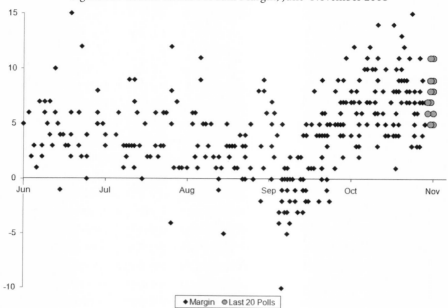

greater from June to October than in the final week (the standard deviation of the residuals, a measurement of the spread of points around the trend line, falls from 2.79 for the black points from June to October to 1.77 for the last twenty polls in gray). David Moore has offered several theories for this "convergence mystery,"[14] but whatever the explanation, *something* about either voter attitudes or pollster methods was clearly different in the final week before the 2008 election. Assuming, as many pollsters do, that this phenomenon was not unique to 2008,[15] how useful are the points in gray from any *prior* election in helping us assess the "accuracy" of the black points for the *next* one?

So what do we do? How can we evaluate new polling results when we see them? The key issue here is, in a way, about faith. Not religious faith per se but faith in random sampling. If we have a true random probability sample, we can have a high degree of confidence that the poll is representative of the larger population. That fundamental philosophy guides most pollsters. The problem for telephone polling today is that many of the assumptions of true probability sampling are breaking down.[16] That change does not mean that polls are suddenly *non*representative, but it does make for a much greater *potential* than ten or twenty years ago for skewed, fluky samples.

What we need is some way to assess whether individual poll samples are truly representative of a larger population that does not rely entirely on faith that "rigorous" methods are in place to make it so. I will grant that this is a very big challenge, one for which I do not have easy answers, especially for the RDD samples of adults typically used for national polls. Since most pollsters already weight adult samples by demographics, the weighted distributions of these variables are inherently representative. But what about other variables like political knowledge, interest, or ideology? Again, I lack easy answers, although, as the quality of voter lists improves in the future, we may get better "auxiliary data" to help identify and correct nonresponse bias.[17] But for now, our options for validating samples are extremely limited.

When it comes to "likely voter" samples, however, pollsters can do far better informing us about whom these polls represent. As reported on Pollster.com and especially on my old Mystery Pollster blog,[18] we have almost as many definitions of likely voters as there are pollsters. Some pollsters use screen questions to identify the likely electorate, some use multiple questions to build indexes that either select likely voters or weight respondents based on their probability of voting. The questions used for this purpose can be about intent to vote, past voting, political interest, or knowledge of voting procedures. Some pollsters select likely voters using official lists of registered voters and the actual turnout information about the individuals selected from those lists. So simply knowing that the pollster has interviewed 600 or 1,000 "likely voters" is not very informative.

The importance of likely voters around elections is obvious, but it is less apparent that many public polls of "likely voters" routinely report on wide variety of policy issues even in nonelection years. These include the polls from Rasmussen Reports, NPR, George Washington University/Battleground and Democracy Corps. What is the most appropriate definition of a "likely voter" in an odd-numbered year? Those who voted or tend to vote in higher turnout presidential elections? Those who intend to vote in nonpresidential elections? Some other definition? The answer is far from obvious.

In five years of blogging, I have learned all too well that many pollsters consider their likely-voter methods proprietary and fiercely resist disclosure of the details. Some will disagree, but I think there are some characteristics that can be disclosed, much like food manufacturers disclose a list of ingredients, without giving away the pollster's "secret sauce." These could include the following:

- In *general terms,* how are likely voters chosen—by screening? Index cutoff models? Weights? Voter file/vote history selection?
- What percentage of the adult population does the likely-voter sample represent?
- If questions were used to screen respondents or build an index, what is the text of questions asked?
- If voter lists were used, what sort of vote history (in general terms if necessary) defined the likely voters?
- Perhaps most important, what is the demographic and attitudinal (party, ideology) profile—weighted and unweighted—of the likely-voter universe?
- Does the pollster provide access to cross-tabulations, especially by party identification?

Unfortunately, obtaining consistent disclosure of such details can be difficult to impossible, depending on the pollster.

How can we help motivate pollsters to disclose more about their methods? Let's consider some recent efforts to improve pollster disclosure and consider an idea to promote more complete transparency in the future.

Consider three efforts to gather details of pollster methods carried out over the past two years. First, in September 2007 on Pollster.com, I made a series of requests of pollsters that had released surveys of likely caucus goers in Iowa.[19] I asked for information about their likely-voter selection methods and for estimates of the percentage of adults represented by their surveys. A month later, seven pollsters—including all but one of the active AAPOR members—had responded fully to my requests. Five, however, provided only partial responses, and five answered none of my questions.[20] I had originally planned to make similar requests regarding polls for the New Hampshire and South Carolina primaries, but the responses trickled in so slowly and required so much individual follow-up that I limited the project to Iowa.

Second, in the wake of the 2008 New Hampshire primary polling snafu, the American Association for Public Opinion Research appointed a committee to investigate the performance of primary polls in New Hampshire and, ultimately, in three other states: South Carolina, California, and Wisconsin. The committee made an extensive request of pollsters, asking not only for information like the AAPOR code requires pollsters to disclose but also for more complete details, including individual-level data for all respondents. Despite allowing pollsters over a year to respond, only seven of twenty-one provided information beyond minimal disclosure. By the time the committee released its report in April 2009 after more than a year's work, three organizations had still failed to respond with even the minimal information mandated by AAPOR's ethical code despite the implicit threat of an AAPOR censure.[21]

Third, starting in August 2008, as part of its "Huffpollstrology" feature, the *Huffington Post* asked a dozen different public pollsters to provide response and refusal rates for their national polls. Six replied with response and refusal rates, two responded with limited calling statistics that did not allow for response rate calculations, and four refused to provide any information about response rates.[22]

The disclosure requirements in the ethical codes of survey organizations like AAPOR and the National Council on Public Polls (NCPP) gained critical mass in the late 1960s. George Gallup, the founder of the Gallup Organization, was a leader in this effort, according to Albert Golin's chapter in a published history of AAPOR.[23] In 1967, Gallup proposed creating what would ultimately become NCPP:

> The disclosure standards [Gallup] was proposing were meant to govern "polling organizations whose findings regularly appear in print and on the air ... also [those] that make private or public surveys for candidates and whose findings are released to the public." It was clear from his prospectus that the prestige of membership (with all that it implied for credentialing) was thought to be sufficient to recruit public polling agencies, while the threat of punitive sanctions (ranging from a reprimand to expulsion) would reinforce their adherence to disclosure standards.[24]

Golin adds that Gallup's efforts were aimed at a small number of "black hat" pollsters in the hope of "draw[ing] them into a group that could then exert peer influence over their activities." Ultimately, this vision evolved into AAPOR's Standards for Minimal Disclosure and NCPP's Principles of Disclosure.[25]

Unfortunately, as the experiences of 2008 attest, larger forces have eroded the ability of groups like AAPOR and NCPP to exert peer pressure on the field. A new breed of pollsters has emerged that cares little about the "prestige of membership" in these groups. Last year, nearly half the surveys we reported at Pollster.com had no sponsor other than the businesses that conducted them. These companies either disseminate polling results in order to promote their companies, make their money by selling subscription access to their data, or both. They know that the demand for new horse race results will drive traffic to their Web sites and expose their brand on cable television news networks. They see little benefit to membership in organizations like NCPP and AAPOR and little need for exposure in more traditional, mainstream media outlets to disseminate their results.

Some recent comments of Tom Jensen, the communications director at Public Policy Polling (PPP), are instructive:

> Perhaps 10 or 20 years ago it would have been a real problem for PPP if our numbers didn't get run in the *Washington Post* but the fact of the matter is people who want to know what the polls are saying are finding out just fine. Every time we've put out a Virginia primary poll we've had three or four days worth of explosion in traffic to both our blog and our main website.[26]

So when pressured by AAPOR, many of these companies feel no need to comply (although I should note for the record that PPP responded to my Iowa queries; it also responded to the AAPOR Ad Hoc Committee request for minimal disclosure, but no more).[27] The process of "punitive sanctions" moves too slowly and often draws too little attention to motivate compliance among non-AAPOR members.

Recently, the AAPOR Standards Committee finally issued a reprimand of one firm, Strategic Vision, LLC, for its lack of disclosure to requests made by the AAPOR Ad Hoc Committee,[28] but the censure came in September 2009 to requests originally made in March 2008. The Strategic Vision case has stirred up media attention, although the resulting controversy probably owed more to the subsequent insinuations by blogger Nate Silver about "the possibility of fraud" by Strategic Vision.[29] The Strategic Vision censure was only AAPOR's second in more than ten years. When it censured a Johns Hopkins researcher for his failure to disclose methodological details in February 2009,[30] the action caused barely a ripple in the news media. (The Memeorandum.com Web site, which compiles dozens of the most tracked news stories on the Internet each day, had not a single reference to the AAPOR censure for the two days following its announcement.)[31]

Meanwhile, the peer pressure that George Gallup envisioned continues to work on responsible AAPOR and NCPP members, leaving them feeling unfairly singled out and exposed to attack by partisans and competitors. I got an earful of this sentiment recently from Keating Holland, the polling director at CNN, as we were both participating in a panel discussion hosted by the Washington, D.C., AAPOR chapter. "Disclosure sounds like a great idea in the confines of a group full of AAPOR people," he said, "but it has real world consequences, *extreme* real world consequences . . . as a general principal, disclosure is a stick you are handing to your enemies and allowing them to beat you over the head with it."

So what do we do? I have an idea, and it's about *scoring* the quality of pollster disclosure.

To explain, let's start with the disclosure information that both AAPOR and NCPP consider mandatory—the information that their codes say should be disclosed in all public reports. While the two standards are not identical, they largely agree on these elements (AAPOR's code describes the release of response rates as mandatory, while NCPP only requires that member pollsters provide this information on request):

- Who sponsored/conducted the survey?
- Dates of interviewing
- Sampling method (e.g., RDD, list, Internet)
- Population (e.g., adults, registered voters, likely voters)
- Sample size
- Size and description of the subsample, if the survey report relies primarily on less than the total sample
- Margin of sampling error

- Survey mode (e.g., live interviewer, automated, Internet, cell phone)
- Complete wording and ordering of questions mentioned in or upon which the release is based
- Percentage results of all questions reported
- [AAPOR only] The AAPOR response rate or a sample disposition report

NCPP goes further and spells out a second level of disclosure—information pertaining to publicly released results that its members should provide on written request:

- Estimated coverage of target population
- Respondent selection procedure (e.g., within household), if any
- Maximum number of attempts to reach respondent
- Exact wording of introduction (any words preceding the first question)
- Complete wording of questions (per Level I disclosure) in any foreign languages in which the survey was conducted
- Weighted and unweighted size of any subgroup cited in the report
- Minimum number of completed questions to qualify a completed interview
- Whether interviewers were paid or unpaid (if live interviewer survey mode)
- Details of any incentives or compensation provided for respondent participation
- Description of weighting procedures (if any) used to generalize data to the full population
- Sample dispositions adequate to compute contact, cooperation, and response rates

NCPP also has a third level of disclosure that "strongly encourages" members to "release raw datasets" for publicly released results and "post complete wording, ordering and percentage results of all publicly released survey questions to a publicly available web site for a minimum of two weeks."[32]

The relatively limited nature of the mandatory disclosure items made sense given the print and broadcast media into which public polls were disseminated when these standards were created. But now, as survey researcher Jan Werner pointed out to me via e-mail, things are different:

When I argued in past decades for fuller disclosure, the response was always that broadcast time or print space were limited resources and too valuable to waste on details that were only of interest to a few specialists. The Internet has now removed whatever validity that excuse may once have had, but we still don't get much real information about polls conducted by the news media, including response rates.

So here is my idea: Make a list of all the elements above, adding the likely-voter information I described earlier in this chapter. Gather and record *whatever methodological information pollsters choose to publicly release* in our database for every public poll that Pollster.com collects. Then use the disclosed data to *score the quality of disclosure of every public survey release.* Aggregation of these scores would allow us to rate the quality of disclosure for each organization and publish the scores alongside polling results.

Now imagine what could happen if we published such disclosure scores on Pollster.com and made them freely available to other Web sites, especially the popular poll aggregators like RealClearPolitics, FiveThirtyEight and the Polling Report. What if all these sites routinely reported disclosure quality scores with polling results the way they do the margin of error? The proliferation of such scores could create a set of incentives for pollsters to improve the quality of their disclosure in a way that enhances their reputations instead of making them feel as if they are handing a club to their enemies.

Imagine further the potential of a database made freely available for noncommercial use (through Creative Commons license) of not just poll results, sample sizes, and survey dates but also a truly rich set of the methodological data disclosed for each survey. Such a resource would provide the raw data for meta-analyses that could enable pollsters to redefine their best practices and the next wave of Nate Silvers to determine which polls are most worthy of our trust.

An added benefit is that this system would not require badgering of pollsters or a reliance on slow and limited punitive sanctions. It would also not place undue emphasis on any one element of disclosure (as *Huffington Post* does with its "Huffpollstrology" feature with response rates). We would record whatever is in the public domain, and if pollsters want to improve their scores, they have some discretion about what new or additional information they choose to release. If a particular element is especially burdensome, they can skip it.

To be sure, the task of creating and publishing disclosure scores is complex and will require considerable resources. The scoring procedure will need to be thought out very carefully, since different types of polls may require different kinds of disclosure. We will need to structure and weight the index so that different categories of polls get scored fairly. I am certain that to succeed, any such project will need considerable input from pollsters and from academics who study survey methodology. The index and scoring procedures will need to be utterly transparent. The information used to score each poll will need to be published on the Internet so that anyone can see it.

This notion may be, for the moment at least, little more than a fanciful idea, but it at least suggests a course to a more objective approach to assessing surveys. "Transparency," argues technologist David Weinberger, "is the new objectivity."[33] When it comes to surveys, it may be the path to trustworthiness as well.

NOTES

1. American Association for Public Opinion Research, "What Is a Random Sample?" www.aapor.org/What_is_a_Random_Sample_.htm (accessed April 9, 2010).

2. Mark Blumenthal, "Huffington's Unintended Gift To Polling," *National Journal Online,* August 3, 2009, www.nationaljournal.com/njonline/po_20090803_7647.php (accessed April 9, 2010).

3. Rasmussen Reports, "Methodology," www.rasmussenreports.com/public_content/about_us/methodology (accessed April 9, 2010).

4. Michael W. Traugott, "Auto-Dialing for Data: A Reply to Scott Rasmussen," *Public Perspective* 11 (2000): 34.

5. The American Association for Public Opinion Research (AAPOR) Ad Hoc Committee on the 2008 Presidential Primary Polling, *AAPOR Committee Report,* www.aapor.org/Report_of_the_AAPOR_Ad_Hoc_Committee_on_the_2008_Presidential_Primary_Polling/1381.htm (accessed April 9, 2009), 9, 28.

6. Nate Silver, "Pollster Ratings," FiveThirtyEight, May 28, 2008, www.fivethirtyeight.com/search/label/pollster%20ratings (accessed April 9, 2010).

7. Nate Silver, "Tracking Poll Primer," FiveThirtyEight, October 21, 2008, www.fivethirtyeight.com/2008/10/tracking-poll-primer.html (accessed April 9, 2010).

8. Mark Blumenthal, "The Hotline Asks Pollsters: What Validates a Poll?" Mystery Pollster, April 22, 2005, www.mysterypollster.com/main/2005/04/the_hotline_ask.html (accessed April 9, 2010).

9. Scott Keeter, Jocelyn Kiley, Leah Christian, and Michael Dimock. "Perils of Polling in Election '08," Pew Research Center, June 25, 2009, www.pewresearch.org/pubs/1266/polling-challenges-election-08-success-in-dealing-with (accessed April 9, 2010).

10. Mark Blumenthal, "Is Polling As We Know It Doomed?" *National Journal Online,* August 10, 2009, www.nationaljournal.com/njonline/mp_20090810_1804.php (accessed April 9, 2010).

11. See Silver, "Pollster Ratings," for these 2008 ratings.

12. Keeter et al., "Perils of Polling in Election '08."

13. For a description of the problem, see Charles Franklin, "From Poll Margins to Wins: Polls as Predictors," Pollster.com, November 6, 2009, www.pollster.com/blogs/from_poll_margin_to_wins_polls.php (accessed April 9, 2010); Joseph Shipman and Jay Leve, "An Interval Measure of Poll Accuracy," www.surveyusa.com/ROR/SurveyUSA%20Interval%20Measure%20of%20Election%20Poll%20Accuracy.html (accessed April 9, 2010); and Carl Bialek, "The Numbers Guy: Grading the Pollsters," *Wall Street Journal Online,* www.online.wsj.com/article/SB116360961928023945.html (accessed April 9, 2010).

14. David Moore, "Evaluating the 2008 Pre-Election Polls—The Convergence Mystery," *Survey Practice,* November 25, 2008, www.surveypractice.org/2008/11/25/a-question-for-the-experts-evaluating-the-2008-pre-election-polls-%E2%80%93-the-convergence-mystery/ (accessed April 9, 2010); David Moore, "The Fluctuating Convergence Mystery," Pollster.com, December 8, 2008, www.pollster.com/blogs/the_fluctuating_convergence_my.php (accessed April 9, 2010); Mark Blumenthal, "More on the 'Convergence Mystery,'" Pollster.com, December 5, 2008, www.pollster.com/blogs/more_on_the_convergence_myster.php (accessed April 9, 2010); Mark Blumenthal, ""Hitting a Bullet with a Bullet"—A Cautionary Tale," Pollster.com, December 23, 2008. www.pollster.com/blogs/hitting_a_bullet_with_a_bullet.php (accessed April 9, 2010).

15. Paul Lavrakas, Michael Traugott, Michelene Blum, Cliff Zukin, and Don Dresser, "The Experts Reply on the Poll Convergence Mystery," *Survey Practice,* December 19, 2008, www.surveypractice.org/2008/12/19/the-experts-reply-convergence-mystery/ (accessed April 9, 2010).

16. Blumenthal, "Is Polling As We Know It Doomed?"

17. Blumenthal, "Huffington's Unintended Gift to Polling."

18. "Likely Voters" (Category Archive), Pollster.com, www.pollster.com/blogs/likely_voters/ (accessed April 9, 2010); Mark Blumethal, "How Do Pollsters Select "Likely Voters?" Mystery Pollster, www.mysterypollster.com/main/2004/09/how_do_pollster_1.html (accessed April 9, 2010).

19. Mark Blumenthal, "The Pollster.com Disclosure Project," Pollster.com, September 24, 2007, www.pollster.com/blogs/the_pollstercom_disclosure_pro.php (accessed April 9, 2010).

20. Mark Blumenthal, "Disclosure Project: Results from Iowa," Pollster.com, December 12, 2007, www.pollster.com/blogs/disclosure_project_results_fro.php (accessed April 9, 2010); Mark Blumenthal, "Disclosure Project: Which Iowa Pollsters Responded?" Pollster.com, October 21, 2007, www.pollster.com/blogs/disclosure_project_which_iowa.php (accessed April 9, 2010).

21. Mark Blumenthal, "AAPOR's Report: Why 2008 Was Not 1948," Pollster.com, September 9, 2009, www.pollster.com/blogs/aapors_report_why_2008_was_not.php (accessed April 9, 2010); AAPOR Ad Hoc Committee on the 2008 Presidential Primary Polling, *An Evaluation of the Methodology of the 2008 Pre-Election Primary Polls,* American Association for Public Opinion Research, March 30, 2009, www.aapor.org/uploads/AAPOR_Rept_FINAL-Rev-4-13-09.pdf (accessed April 9, 2010).

22. "Huffpollstrology," *Huffington Post,* www.huffingtonpost.com/tag/huffpollstrology (accessed April 9, 2010); Mark Blumenthal, "Huffington's Unintended Gift to Polling."

23. Paul Sheatsley, *A Meeting Place: The History of the American Association for Public Opinion Research* ([Ann Arbor, MI]: AAPOR, 1992), www.aapor.org/Content/NavigationMenu/AboutAAPOR/History/AMeetingPlaceAAPORHistoryBook/default.htm (accessed July 20, 2010).

24. Ibid.

25. American Association for Public Opinion Research, "Disclosure Standards," www.aapor.org/Disclosure_Standards.htm (accessed April 9, 2010); National Council on Public Polls, "Principles of Disclosure," www.ncpp.org/?q=node/19 (accessed April 9, 2010).

26. Tom Jensen, "Polling in Virginia," Public Policy Polling, May 18, 2009, www.publicpolicypolling.blogspot.com/2009/05/polling-in-virginia.html (accessed April 9, 2010).

27. AAPOR Ad Hoc Committee on the 2008 Presidential Primary Polling, *Evaluation of the Methodology.*

28. AAPOR, "AAPOR Raises Objections to Actions by Atlanta-Based Strategic Vision LLC," www.aapor.org/AAPOR_Raises_Objections_to_Actions_by_Strategic_Vision_LLC.htm (accessed April 9, 2010).

29. Nate Silver, "Pollster Ratings."

30. AAPOR, "AAPOR Finds Gilbert Burnham in Violation of Ethics Code," February 4, 2009, www.aapor.org/AAPOR_Finds_Gilbert_Burnham_in_Violation_of_Ethics_Code/1383.htm (accessed April 9, 2010).

31. "memeorandum @ 8:00 PM ET, February 4, 2009," February 4, 2009, www.memeorandum.com/090204/h2000; "memeorandum @ 8:00 PM ET, February 5, 2009," February 5, 2009, www.memeorandum.com/090205/h2000 (accessed April 9, 2010).

32. National Council on Public Polls, "Principles of Disclosure."

33. David Weinberger, "Transparency Is the New Objectivity," *Supernova Hub,* August 9, 2009, www.supernovahub.com/2009/08/transparency-is-the-new-objectivity/ (accessed April 9, 2010).

4

Poll-Centered News Coverage

Causes and Consequences

JOHANNA DUNAWAY

If the accuracy of polls is increasingly in question, why do they play such a prominent role in news coverage of campaigns and policy? As several of the preceding chapters note, we are faced with a poll-inundated information environment wherein polls of varying types and quality are available to the public with little or no filtering. The result is a "perfect storm" of growing public and media reliance on an increasing array of public opinion polls, many of which may use questionable methods and provide misinformation.

Chapter 1 presented the following paradox: despite increasing challenges facing survey research and increased skepticism about the credibility of polls, there is greater demand for polls and more people conducting them. This chapter examines a different paradox: Why has news coverage of poll results increased even as the credibility of polls is increasingly in question? First, why is news coverage of polls increasing and under what circumstances do we see an increase in poll-centered news coverage? Second, if we are seeing less scrutiny and less sophisticated news analysis of polls, why is this? Third, are polls used instead of expert/thoughtful commentary or hard news coverage of issues? If so, when and why? Finally, what potential harm might these trends do to the public's understanding of politics? More generally, what problems might these trends create for democracy?

The focus of this volume is the meaning and measurement of public opinion in a digital age. Although the questions posed above are broad, this chapter examines them in light of changes to the news media environment spurred by the evolution of the modern communication environment. The aim is to provide some leverage on the question posed in the introductory chapter, "How does a changing media system challenge the measurement and interpretation of public opinion?"

Why Is News Coverage of Polls Increasing?

Let's begin with a simple proposition: Despite growing concerns about their accuracy, news coverage of opinion polls has increased in recent years.[1] While one might think of a number of reasons for this, most have to do with the changing nature of the polls themselves or a change in the norms and routines in news coverage of polls (and politics).

Kirby Goidel, Susan Herbst, and Mark Blumenthal each describe the general proliferation of polls in the field, which means the sheer increase in the number of polls could naturally generate more poll-centered news coverage. Mark Blumenthal further notes the "publicity value" to polling firms when their polls are covered in the news. Blumenthal describes how many private polling firms are little concerned with professional reputation as long as they can manipulate the demand for horse race news and get their polls aired and their polling firm advertised. This publicity is reason enough for polling firms to generate press releases, post their results on the Web, and find other ways to encourage news media to cover their results.

In addition, several *specific* circumstances brought on by changes in the media environment have compounded the problem of news media presenting a disproportionate amount of poll-centered news stories relative to the larger campaign context. For example, it is generally accepted that declining ad revenue and increased competition have led to extensive newsroom cutbacks in news organizations around the country.[2] Empirical evidence suggests that both market pressures and newsroom cutbacks increase coverage of polls, especially during elections. Shanto Iyengar's research demonstrates that voters and audiences prefer horse race news stories to stories covering public policy issues, and additional research finds that newsrooms with reduced political reporting staffs and news outlets in competitive markets provide less coverage of policy issues during campaigns.[3]

These market pressures and newsroom cutbacks are related to changes in the media environment that have occurred with the arrival of the "digital age." First, the arrival of new information technology has resulted in a general proliferation of news outlets. Two decades ago, the national media landscape was dominated by the three major television networks, papers like the *New York Times* and the *Washington Post,* and the larger wire services such as the Associated Press. Since that time, the media environment has expanded to include scores of new outlets; among the newest are political Web blogs and news Web sites available on the Internet. The arrival and proliferation of these "new players" have had several important consequences for the news media and have led to an increase in the production of poll-centered news stories.

Tom Rosenstiel describes three changes to our media culture that are important for our understanding of why poll coverage is increasing.[4] First, in recent years there have been widespread newsroom cutbacks brought about by increased competition and ad revenue lost in the audience flight to digital news. Second, the multiplayer nature of today's media culture has produced a heavy reliance on secondhand news material in lieu of original reporting. Third, the gradual arrival of scores of new outlets and new technology has led to a demand for twenty-four-hour news.

With regard to newsroom cutbacks and an increase in poll reporting, the relationship is straightforward. As Kirby Goidel notes in Chapter 1, "For newspapers with declining circulations, revenue, and staff, opinion polls provide an easy story line or narrative to frame political developments and breaking events." This logic also applies to television news coverage and news Web sites. Perhaps most important, polls are utilized more heavily in the context of newsroom cutbacks. Because poll results require little editing or interpreting, many outlets take them directly from the wire copy with little adaptation. In short, poll result stories are used more often in newsrooms with cutback-reduced staffs because they are simple and require little work, they have audience appeal, they are timely, and they are immediately available without utilizing scarce resources.[5]

The second change brought about by the digitalization of information and the proliferation of news outlets is the increased demand for secondhand material. The fact that there are more players and more technology in the media field does not necessarily imply there is more original reporting and news gathering. It simply means there are more people and organizations delivering news content in various ways. As Tom Rosenstiel has argued, this has translated into more "news aggregators" gathering and delivering news; the growing trend of news aggregation and delivery accelerates the demand for secondhand news material.[6]

Secondhand material refers to information gathered outside the reporting news organization (i.e., materials not produced from the original research of the reporting news organization). Information obtained through polls makes excellent secondhand material for several reasons: it fits very well with traditional news values (i.e., it makes a good story); it is timely, easy to understand, and appealing to audiences. Moreover, it is abundant and thus helps satisfy the high demand for secondhand material, and it fits nicely within the commonly used horse race style of election reporting.[7]

Poll data make excellent fodder for the twenty-four-hour news cycle as well. In the days of evening network news dominance, news organizations were only required to prepare stories for newscasts aired a few times a day. Similarly, newspapers were only required to provide stories for the morning or evening edition. Now, these news organizations must compete with twenty-four-hour news networks such as CNN, and the Internet makes it possible for them to try to keep up by continually updating posts on their Web sites. Thus, the twenty-four-hour news cycle demands constant material for news stories, which means that, because they cannot hire large news staff in the current media climate, news organizations rely more heavily on information feeds from press releases and wire services. Secondhand material such as poll results from polling firms is just the sort of material to arrive this way—in convenient press results requiring minimal edits. In short, the constant demand for twenty-four-hour news means that, whenever possible, outlets will take free and available poll results that can be easily crafted into a news story.

Are We Seeing Less Scrutiny and Less Sophisticated News Analysis of Polls?

As of yet, no one has produced a systematic study with the specific aim of determining whether news analysis of polls has become less sophisticated with evolving changes to the news media. Yet there is evidence that we are seeing less sophisticated analysis of polls. Drawing from his experience as a reporter and from research in the Project for Excellence in Journalism's annual "State of the News Media" reports, Tom Rosenstiel has described at length the structural trends that have contributed to the now frequent press (mis)use of polling today. These trends are the same ones delineated in the previous section (e.g., newsroom cutbacks, greater reliance on secondhand news material, and greater demand for twenty-four-hour news) that operate to increase the volume of polling coverage. Yet these trends are also discussed here because they have a direct influence on *the ability and willingness of journalists and other news gatherers to provide meticulous analysis of polls.*

Of these trends, newsroom cutbacks have perhaps the most obvious effect on the quality of poll analysis in news coverage. First, newsroom cutbacks have resulted in fewer reporters available to cover the news, fewer reporting hours, and fewer individuals dedicated to the planning and research behind political news stories. Second, the cutbacks have largely played out in terms of newsroom layoffs and buyouts. Because senior, more experienced reporters have higher salaries, they are often the first targets of such measures. While young reporters might be available for less cost, they also have less experience. In the current cost-cutting environment, those posting polls to the Web site or writing about them are less likely to have a background in political reporting. In short, newsrooms reeling from cutbacks lack the time, personnel, expertise, and experience required to provide sophisticated analysis of the opinion polls they cover.

The greater reliance on secondhand news material also influences the sophistication of poll coverage. This reliance (brought about in part by newsroom cutbacks) means that news organizations are more willing to use polls from unfamiliar sources and with limited information about the credibility of the work. In addition, newsroom cutbacks mean there are fewer people to produce original stories to run in lieu of polling stories, and fewer news staff workers around to independently verify the credibility of the polling organization or given poll results.

Compounding these problems is the current media environment's demand for twenty-four-hour news. In much the same way the current news cycle promulgated an increase in opinion poll coverage more generally, it also affects the sophistication of reporters' polling analysis. The twenty-four-hour news hole is so big, it not only demands a reliance on more polls but increases the tendency to use lax standards when choosing whether and how to run a poll story. Rosenstiel puts it this way: "There is frankly more news time to fill than there is news to fill it. As such there is more appetite for the latest poll, the latest anything, further making the press less discriminating. Against this backdrop, more polls means more stuff to put on the site or on the air."[8]

Clearly, the need for constant and timely news material often outweighs the preference for a high-quality news product. Thus, reports are often rushed or offered without context or background. The twenty-four-hour news demand also increases the tendency to air stories about polls released from the less reputable polling firms, in which case the reporting news organization might opt not to provide more in-depth analysis to avoid revealing low response rates or large margins of error.

Are Polls Used Instead of Expert/Thoughtful Commentary or Hard News Coverage?

In an attempt to answer this question, this section uses election data, news industry data, and newspaper content in an exploratory analysis to try to predict the various factors that influence news organizations' use of horse race poll coverage in statewide elections.[9] Specifically, the analysis attempts to explain the incidence of poll coverage in statewide elections as function of election characteristics (electoral competition), news organization characteristics (number of political reporters, market penetration, ownership structure, and circulation), and market demographics (percentage college educated and percentage 55 and older).

As the arguments presented in this chapter suggest, newsroom cutbacks and market competition should influence the degree to which news organizations rely on horse race coverage of polls in lieu of more substantive coverage. Specifically, the probability that a given news story will include horse race coverage of polls should increase when (1) the news organization is owned by a major corporation or chain; (2) its share of the market is relatively low; and (3) there are fewer political reporters on staff to provide alternative content. To test these propositions, the analysis relies on media content from 1,852 election-oriented news stories covering a mix of guber-

Table 4.1.

Logistic Regression Estimates, Horse Race Polling Coverage

	Variables	Coefficients (Standard errors)
Organizational factors	Ownership	.245
		(0.210)
	Market penetration	-0.015^{***}
		(0.004)
	Number of political reporters	$-.068^{**}$
		(0.028)
	Circulation	$.503^{***}$
		(0.129)
Electoral factors	Electoral competition	.019
		(.032)
	Female candidate	.287
		(.264)
Market factors	% in market with college degree	$-.024^{*}$
		(.017)
	% in market 55+ years of age	.031
		(0.041)
	Constant	-8.91^{***}
		(1.72)

Notes: Robust standard errors in parentheses, clustered on (33) news organizations. P-values reflect 1-tailed tests. $^{*}p < .10$, $^{**}p < .05$, $^{***}p < .01$. N = 1,852.

natorial and Senate elections in 6 U.S. states and across 7 statewide elections and 31 media markets. The news stories analyzed are those that appeared between September 1 and Election Day. The majority of stories in the sample (57 percent) focused on campaign strategy, including horse race stories, but did not include a specific reference to poll results. A smaller percentage (22 percent) of horse race coverage included specific references to poll results.

Notably poll-focused news stories were more frequent than issue stories (14 percent of coverage) or candidate characteristics (3 percent), and collectively poll-focused news stories contribute to the predominance of horse race coverage in statewide elections. In Table 4.1, we present the results of a logistic regression that allows us to test whether poll-focused news coverage differs systematically across news organizations, electoral contexts, and market demographics. Computationally, logistic regression is quite complex. Conceptually, it is much easier to understand. The results of the logistic regression tell us whether news organizations with specific characteristics (e.g., corporate ownership and fewer reporters) are more likely than other news organizations to run poll-focused news stories.

The first variable of interest (ownership) has to do with media consolidation, which has been an additional consequence of the increasingly competitive nature of the changing media landscape. Today, newspapers and television stations are often owned by vast publicly traded corporations or large group ownership chains instead of privately owned independent news organizations. Though the trend toward corporate and chain ownership has been growing for some time, the arrival of digital media accelerated this trend during the past two decades. Extant research has previously demonstrated that news organizations with corporate ownership are less likely to offer substantive issue coverage due to their drive for maximized profits at the behest of shareholders.[10] Thus, we would expect consolidated media ownership (i.e., large media corporations owning scores of outlets) to be positively related to horse race poll coverage, meaning that more consolidated ownership means more horse race coverage. The results presented in Table 4.1, however, reveal that ownership does not affect the probability of poll-focused news coverage. While previous findings have demonstrated a positive and significant relationship between public shareholder ownership and less substantive coverage of policy issues (i.e., corporate ownership leads to less policy coverage), ownership consolidation appears not to be as significant of a predictor for the specific category of polling coverage.

The second variable of interest (market penetration) also has to do with news organization profit seeking and market competition. Market penetration is a commonly used indicator of a newspaper's financial well-being; it is measured as the percentage of households that subscribe to the newspaper against the total number of households in the newspaper market area. Since horse race coverage has the most audience appeal when compared with other types of election news stories, newspapers with less of a market share (i.e., more threatened by competition) will be more likely to rely on this widely appealing coverage in an effort to attract a larger audience. Table 4.1 indeed indicates that market penetration is negative related to the incidence of polling-focused news stories. The smaller a paper's market share, the more profit driven it becomes as it tries to gain a foothold in the market; the larger the market share, the less often it must rely on horse race coverage to draw an audience. A larger market share also probably means more resources, which translates into more substantial reporting in lieu of simple poll coverage.

Figure 4.1 provides a graphical illustration of the relationship between market penetration and polling coverage using predicted probability estimates. These estimates are useful because they show differences in the probability that a given news story will include polling coverage at different levels of newspaper market penetration while holding all the other variables constant at their mean values. What Figure 4.1 reveals is that when a paper has a low level of market penetration, there is a 5 percent chance that any given election story will include polling coverage, while at medium and high levels of market penetration there is only a 3 percent and 2 percent chance of seeing polling coverage, respectively.

The third variable of interest (number of political reporters) addresses the size of the reporting staff that is dedicated to reporting news about politics, and it is measured as the number of political reporters on staff. As one might expect from the prior discussion about the relationship between newsroom cutbacks and reliance on poll coverage, Table 4.1 verifies that the number of political reporters on staff is significantly and negatively related to poll-centered coverage. This means that the fewer reporters in a newspaper available to cover politics, the higher the probability of poll-focused news stories. Alternatively, this finding supports the idea that having more political reporters on staff leads to less reliance on superficial and often unreliable poll coverage. Figure 4.2 provides a graph of the probability estimates for polling coverage based on the size of the political reporting staff. As Figure 4.2 shows, holding all else constant, news organizations with large political reporting staffs have less than a 1 percent probability of offering poll stories.

Figure 4.1. Probability of Horserace Poll Stories by Market Penetration

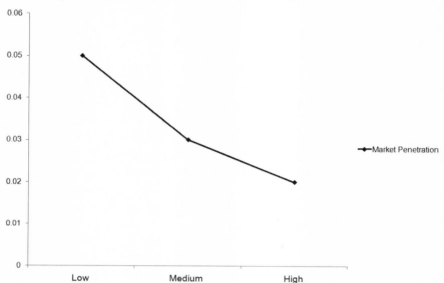

Alternatively, news organizations with small political reporting staffs have a 4 percent probability of presenting polling stories.

The fourth variable in Table 4.1 (circulation) is a measure of newspaper subscription and is used here as an indicator of newspaper size and resources. Given that the circulation size of a paper likely influences the total number of stories printed and the newsroom budget, it must be included in the model even though the model controls for the size of the political reporting staff. Here, circulation size is positively and significantly related to poll coverage as well. This indicates that circulation has an independent effect on the probability of polling coverage. This suggests that larger newspapers are generally more likely to produce a higher volume of poll-focused news stories.

The next two variables in the model are primarily control variables as well; both control for electoral characteristics that could conceivably influence the probability of poll-focused coverage. The first electoral factor (electoral competition) is an indicator of how competitive the race was between

Figure 4.2. Probability of Horserace Poll Stories by Political Reporting Staff

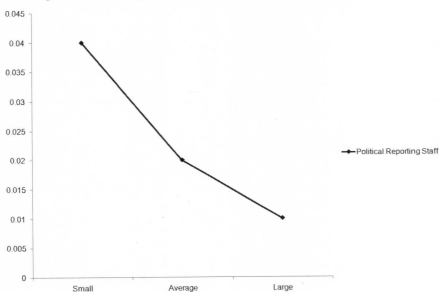

the candidates and is included in the model simply as a control. We would expect less poll coverage for less competitive races because poll stories are more exciting (and therefore more appealing to audiences) when elections are close. The second electoral factor (female candidate) is included because extant research has shown that coverage of races with female political candidates typically contains more of the horse race.[11] Neither electoral control in the model was significantly related to horse race coverage.

Extant research has also revealed that there are audience-related contextual effects on news content.[12] Specifically, market-level indicators of demographics such as education, income, age, ideology, and gender have been found to influence news content because certain demographic groups are known to have particular news preferences.[13] Thus, similar indicators are included here so that we can explore whether these characteristic might directly influence horse race polling coverage specifically. These include market-level indicators for education (percentage with college degree) and age (percentage 55 and older). These particular demographics were included because older audiences are known to prefer more substantive news (as suggested by Hamilton), as are the more educated (supported by Dunaway's research). Therefore, we could expect that older and more educated audiences would prefer less superficial horse race poll coverage and more substantive policy-related coverage, which might translate into fewer horse race news offerings in markets with a high percentage of elderly and more educated residents. Here the indicator for older market audiences has a nonsignificant impact on polling stories; the education variable is in the expected negative direction and reaches significance, but only at the .10 level. Markets with more educated populations do receive less horse race coverage, but the relationship is not a strong one.

This exploratory analysis provides some insight about when news organizations are likely to rely heavily on poll-centered news stories in lieu of policy-related election coverage. First, poll-focused coverage is often offered at the expense of more substantive coverage, just as some extant research suggests.[14] Moreover, it is clear that there are particular circumstances under which this is most likely to happen, largely based on the structure of news organizations and their competitive position within their media market.

All together, news organizations most concerned about competition and profit are the ones most likely to rely heavily on poll-oriented news stories at the expense of more substantive stories. Alternatively, news organizations with a more comfortable market position and those dedicating more resources to political reporting are least likely to rely so heavily on poll-centered horse race stories. In sum, the analysis makes clear that any and all profit- or competition-related changes to the media culture brought about by the arrival of the digital age (e.g., more competitors, loss of audience to online news) have direct and important influences on the pervasiveness of disproportionate poll-centered election coverage and the problems therein. These problems are discussed in further detail in the next section.

What Potential Harm Might These Trends Cause to Public Understanding of Politics?

In Chapter 1, readers were asked to consider this question: Should polls play such a prominent role when the credibility of polling is increasingly in doubt? While the clear answer for many would be no, the current situation does not provide an obvious solution. Disproportionate coverage of polling is largely due to market considerations because "horserace stories elicit greater public attention than policy stories."[15] This means that as news organizations face steeper competition from multiple venues they will be more likely to trade substance for audience appeal. In terms of election coverage, this will translate into more poll-centered horse race stories and fewer issue-focused stories. As the analysis presented here shows, horse race coverage of polling is harmful because it crowds out several different types of more substantive coverage. This conclusion is also supported by findings from Iyengar, Norpoth, and Hahn, who note that poll-driven horse race reporting erodes citizens' understanding of politics and that the "over-production of horse-race news means that citizens will be less likely to encounter 'substantive' information about the candidates and issues."[16] Additionally, the more news organizations rely on polls to frame their news stories, Rosentiel suggests, the more likely they will be to use relaxed standards when choosing which polls warrant coverage. In short, the current for-profit structure of our media coupled with the technology-driven economic challenges news organizations face will continue to foster high demand for all polls regardless of their perceived (or real) credibility.

What Problems Might These Trends Create for Democracy?

From a democratic standpoint, it is useful to think about what variations in news content are important for politics and for citizens' use in making political judgments. One factor seems to have particular importance in this regard: whether the information in news content is sufficient to allow the comparison of candidates and issue positions. When viewed in this light, news quality refers to the amount of substantive policy, government, and candidate information provided in news content. Unfortunately, the discussion and analysis in this chapter suggest that poll-centered coverage is nonsubstantive, on the rise, and even crowding out more substantive coverage. Consequently, it seems that the disproportionate emphasis on poll-centered news coverage brought on by the digital age poses problems for the pool of information available to citizens for democratic decision making.

NOTES

1. Andrew Kohut, "Polls," in *The Politics of News, the News of Politics*, 2nd ed., ed. Doris A. Graber, Denis McQuail, and Pippa Norris, 150–70 (Washington, DC: CQ Press, 2006).

2. Pew Project for Excellence in Journalism, "The State of the News Media," www.stateofthe-media.org/2010/ (accessed April 9, 2010).

3. Shanto Iyengar, Helmut Norpoth, and Kyu S. Hahn, "Consumer Demand for Election News: The Horserace Sells," *Journal of Politics* 66 (2004): 157–75; Johanna Dunaway, "Markets, Ownership, and the Quality of Campaign News Coverage," *Journal of Politics* 70 (2008): 1193–1202.

4. Tom Rosenstiel, "Political Polling and the New Media Culture: A Case of More Being Less," *Public Opinion Quarterly* 69 (2005): 698–715.

5. Iyengar, Norpoth, and Hahn, "Consumer Demand for Election News."

6. Rosenstiel, "Political Polling and the New Media Culture."

7. Iyengar, Norpoth, and Hahn, "Consumer Demand for Election News."

8. Rosenstiel, "Political Polling and the New Media Culture," 702.

9. The data are from the following elections: Alaska gubernatorial 2006; Colorado Senate 2004, 2008; Louisiana Senate 2008; Nebraska Senate 2008; Rhode Island gubernatorial 2006; and Washington gubernatorial 2004.

10. Dunaway, "Markets, Ownership, and the Quality of Campaign News Coverage."

11. Kim F. Kahn, *The Political Consequences of Being a Woman: How Stereotypes Influence the Conduct and Consequences of Political Campaigns* (New York: Columbia University Press, 1996).

12. James Hamilton, *All the News That's Fit to Sell: How the Market Transforms Information into News* (Princeton: Princeton University Press, 2004); Dunaway, "Markets, Ownership, and the Quality of Campaign News Coverage."

13. Matthew Gentzkow and Jesse M. Shapiro, "What Drives Media Slant? Evidence from U.S. Daily Newspapers" (Working Paper No. 12707, National Bureau of Economic Research, 2006).

14. In the total sample of news stories, the categories broke down as follows: 14 percent issue coverage, 3 percent coverage of candidate characteristics, 5 percent adwatch stories (stories that break down the accuracy of candidate claims in political ads), 57 percent strategy stories (horse race or game frame stories not focusing primarily on poll results), and 22 percent horse race poll stories (stories wherein the primary focus was poll results). Percentages don't add up to exactly 100 percent due to rounding.

15. Iyengar, Norpoth, and Hahn, "Consumer Demand for Election News," 160.

16. Ibid., 158.

5

(Un)Numbered Voices?

Reconsidering the Meaning of Public Opinion in a Digital Age

SUSAN HERBST

It is a common irony that the concepts we view as fundamental to democracy are the very ones we find nearly impossible to define. For hundreds of years, statesmen and scholars have debated the meanings of "representation" and "citizenship," for example, coming to their own conclusions but certainly not settling the issues. "Public opinion" falls into this category, and if we had to rank our nebulous concepts, it would be near the top of any list.

While this is aggravating to some of us, hoping to develop shared language, it is stimulating as well: the meaning of public opinion is both enormously complex and endlessly in transition. So, in keeping with the spirit of this rocky evolution, I will take a very quick tour though some vital moments in Western history but then focus on where we are in the American year of 2010. How do our current circumstances—cultural, economic, and technological—affect the ways we think about public opinion? What challenges—worrisome and welcome—has the Internet brought to the fairly conventional social scientific field of public opinion research?

The Historical Evolution of "Public Opinion"

Public opinion and related concepts (e.g., the "public sentiment," the "climate of opinion," the "voice of the people") have been with us for a very long time, and in scrutinizing them, we stand on the shoulders of many giants—Wilhelm Bauer, Paul Lazarsfeld, and of course, Jurgen Habermas.[1] The ancient Greeks and Romans were intensely interested in public opinion and wrote about it in a variety of ways, still of great use to political theorists, rhetoricians, and others. Yet many social historians track the phrase "public opinion," as well as the heightened interest in public sentiments, to eighteenth-century Paris, seeing it as part of the Enlightenment discourse. The philosopher Jean-Jacques Rousseau and the far more practical Jacques Necker, finance minister to Louis XVI, are sometimes credited with coining the phrase "l'opinion publique." While they are both profoundly interesting and brilliant historical figures, Necker was the political player, Rahm Emanuel–like, given his responsibilities to the court and citizenry. As historian Paul Palmer pointed out in 1936, well before Habermas produced his work on the appearance of a public sphere in France, public opinion emerged as an idea embedded in a community: intellectuals, statesmen, artists, and other elites of the eighteenth century had begun to develop arenas for the exchange of ideas, to assert their power to question the king, and to develop a self-consciousness for the people.[2]

Necker articulated the notion of public opinion with force, seeing it as "an invisible power which, without treasures, without a bodyguard, and without an army gives laws to the city, to the court, and even to the palaces of kings."[3] Necker, like so many leaders of his time, frequented the nightly salons run by brilliant Parisian women in their homes—gatherings designed for social and political critique, for discussions of religion and art, and for sexual intrigue. Most important, the salons were the birthplace of revolutionary thought in the heady days before the blood and terror of social change to come.[4] While the eighteenth-century French, British, Germans, and various other European intellectuals contributed to the notion of a "public"—with its own independence of thought and expression—it would be difficult to argue that there was debate about the meaning of "public opinion." Although public opinion (conceptual and real) would be fundamental to the great revolutions, and to evolving notions of democracy, there was not so much actual grappling with it. Public opinion was still a rather nebulous, if important, idea, and little thought was given to assessing it or measuring it in any contemporary sense. Public opinion was seen as located in salons, coffeehouses, political tracts, reports of court cases, novels, plays, and, later, the pages of newspapers. But wherever one found public opinion, it was somehow tied to *talk*—not to counting people, ideas, or election returns (there were no general elections). Public opinion was embedded in communities, elite ones like salons very often but in the far more plebian coffeehouses of London as well. Even with the emergence of the newspaper, public opinion was a *conversational* concept: eighteenth- and nineteenth-century citizens did not tromp out to their driveways to snatch up a newspaper for private reading. Newspapers were products of taverns and coffeehouses, read aloud and passing through many hands, much the same way northern African American newspapers circulated in early twentieth-century southern barbershops.[5]

If we advance across the Atlantic to nineteenth-century America, the essential tie between public opinion and conversation is evident and powerful as well. Alexis de Tocqueville and James Bryce, two visitors who wrote extensively about public opinion in the mid- and late nineteenth century, documented the meetings, assemblies, and less formal exchanges that characterized public opinion at the time. Reading their great works (*Democracy in America* and *The American Commonwealth*, respectively) underscores the dialogic nature of public opinion.

But while conversation—talk in public or private about the social and political issues of the day—was an anchor of American culture, another strand of human inclination was developing at an accelerated pace: the desire to count. As Patricia Cline Cohen put it so well, Americans have a tendency toward quantification and are, in fact, a "calculating people."[6] Given this numerical sensibility, and the momentum of positivism, the late nineteenth and early twentieth centuries saw a rise in elections, electioneering, and straw polling.

Straw polling, an incredibly popular American pastime of the nineteenth century, had been a human endeavor since the ancient democracies: we seek to understand the opinions of others and have a natural interest in majorities and minorities. Aggregating votes or opinions is commonplace in democracies but also in nations or regions where dictators hope to depress public opinion and avoid the emergence of a democratic polity. All of this was well understood in the nineteenth century. And along with straw polls of the period, we should not forget the time-honored petition, a practice of opinion quantification begun by the English but greeted with open arms in the United States.[7]

Conversation versus Counting?

A key question for historians of public opinion, one that has kept us busy for decades, is how the drive toward quantification and the basis of public opinion in conversation are intertwined. I posit here that we can find, in every epoch, a subterranean struggle between these two approaches to public opinion: public opinion as an aggregation of individual opinions and public opinion as a nonquantified but powerful conversation. It is never one or the other; that would make mapping the history of public opinion easy. The point is that all people struggle with the fundamental epistemological question of how to best to know, understand, and measure the opinions of others. So much depends on our tools, our priorities, our roles, our values, and our moment in time. To the busy network executive during a presidential election season, polling—aggregating individual opinion as best we can and as quickly as we can—seems appropriate, intelligent, and entertaining to an audience caught in the horse race. But for the senator hoping to pursue environmental legislation for the long-term health of his or her state, or the leader of a minority interest group seeking to build strategy, the actual dynamics of the public conversation may be more important and more determinative of how they will lead, talk, and act.

One of my favorite moments of struggle in the history of public opinion, an instance where the difficulty of defining public opinion is clear to scholars, at least, is the reports from the Second National Conference on the Science of Politics, held in Chicago in the autumn of 1924.[8] In panels similar to our current-day American Political Science Association convention panels, leading researchers gathered to discuss the prominent questions in the field and debate future directions. At a roundtable titled "The Measurement of Public Opinion," a variety of distinguished scholars gathered to articulate definitions of "opinion" and to discuss the conditions under which opinions are public ones (as opposed to private opinions). Debate ensued, and A. N. Holcombe—a scholar who would go on to serve as APSA president in 1936—eventually noted:

> After some discussion . . . it was agreed that an exact definition of
> public opinion might not be needed until after the technical problem
> of measuring the opinions of the individual members of the public

had been disposed of. It was decided therefore that the round table might well proceed to consider the problem of measuring opinion, especially that relating to political matters, and avoid the use of the term public opinion, if possible.[9]

This is interesting to us on many levels. In 1924, American political scientists saw the United States as an already highly evolved democracy, one with a storied past and tremendous stability. The problems of America—segregation, poverty, labor strife, our complex European entanglements—were obvious, but the political system with its two major parties and occasional challenges seemed to "work." Hence, throughout the 1924 discussions there is a sort of calm, and even smugness, about public opinion. Perhaps it did not seem so at the meeting, but to my mind, dismissing the central issue—a need to define public opinion—and simply turning to quantitative measurement instead seems a rather major cop-out. Why so little struggle about who constitutes the public and about the nature of having an opinion? Was the busy young field of political science so industrious that its leaders viewed these as annoying philosophical matters, to be avoided as unproductive? Was it an avoidance of the real divides in American society—race, class, education, religion—that might make "public opinion" difficult to confront for these researchers? Or was it the simple desire of a group of well-meaning, collegial scholars to just make some practical progress? We will never know the sensibility of that moment, over eighty-five years ago, but one thing is clear: there was no shared meaning of public opinion at all, only a real recognition of how nebulous the concept had become.

It would be difficult to say that this 1924 conference was a "seminal moment" or turning point, but it is around this period that measurement of public opinion, through surveying, began to take off in ways that no one could have imagined. The *Literary Digest* preelection polling became enormously popular, and the 1930s saw the rise of George Gallup and other great pollsters of the mid-twentieth century. They honed their predictive tools with much success. While they built the political polling and market research industries, on the drive to profit (a point often largely overlooked in most histories of polling), some of the more thoughtful pollsters like Gallup opined on the nature of democracy itself. In his polemical *The Pulse of De-*

mocracy, Gallup admits to the imperfection of knowing the human mind in all its complexity. He was a sophisticated man. But he also sells the technique of opinion polling, hard, as the best and most effective means for enabling democracy: How else can the common working man or woman be heard? How can we avoid a "tyranny of the majority" unless we use representative sampling? Gallup sees polling as a commodity useful to anxious legislators but also as a mechanism by which Americans can speak truth to power.

The 1930s were successful years for Gallup and the pollsters, although legislators, presidential candidates, and other elites were not quite ready to cede the measure and understanding of public opinion to the new opinion "scientists." The polling industry was seen as promising but worrisome, throwing a wrench into the way Americans thought about politics. After all, conversation, meetings, and assembly were—as Tocqueville so deftly documented—the heart and soul of American political opinion expression. Where, in the course of opinion polling, was the conversation and debate? If a person is to interview me in confidence about my views, adding them to the anonymous opinions of others and publicizing these for the world to see, where's the dialogue?

These worries were sometimes relayed in public, but mostly not. In fact, the academic critique of opinion polling during the mid-twentieth century was weirdly thin, with only a few standout voices and essays. Paul Lazarsfeld and others occasionally reminded scholars that there are ways to know opinion besides polls—strikes, media content, petitions, and meetings. Lindsay Rogers would similarly observe that "instead of feeling the pulse of democracy, Dr. Gallup listens to its baby talk."[10] But in terms of a direct assault on the new science of opinion polling and what it might mean for both scholarship and American society, there is a dearth of discourse. The reason seems clear to me: social scientists are not social theorists, typically, and have limited patience for what they see as higher-brow epistemological debate. We are a practical bunch, and psychometric measurement—capturing attitudes through scaling—was a field of great progress and promise. But I do wonder whether the impatience to just get out there and "do something," regarding opinion measurement, masked a discomfort with the public itself. American public opinion is, and always has been, messy, conflictual, difficult, and full of discrimination and bias. To jump to measurement, instead of pondering the public itself—its attributes both good and bad—was expedient and fitting to an American social science on the move. However, it may not have been in the best interests of a diverse democratic nation.

One man stood out, though, and questioned the tremendous push toward survey research and polling results as a "stand-in" for public opinion. It was 1947, a moment of great progress in the evolving survey research industry, within the academy and beyond. Herbert Blumer, a professor at the University of Chicago and one of the most distinguished sociologists in the nation, was asked to "present observations" at the meetings of the American Sociological Society, which were later published in the *American Sociological Review*.[11] In the essay, still the most thoughtful critique of survey research we have, Blumer argued that polling simply could not serve as a measure of public opinion, as most people understand and value it. His critique included multiple sparring points. He worried that polls were an aggregation of individual opinions that did not map onto the existing power structure: interest groups, ethnic enclaves, and powerful people *make things happen* and are in fact the public opinion of interest to any social scientist. Artificial publics—hundreds of anonymous, unorganized people, not related to each other in any way—have no place in social analysis. The artifice of the sample survey does not "act" and lives as a faceless American cross section, suspended in time, never to be gathered again. How could it possibly be thought of as a meaningful public?

Blumer saw public opinion formation as a process driven by groups and group interests. These are "functional" groups, related to class, race, ethnicity, interest, and other binding characteristics. Not only does polling ignore this infrastructure, he argues. Polling outright defies it and therefore can present us with only the most unsophisticated of political analyses. Polls present us with an illusion; they do not produce meaningful, predictive data about the issue dynamics of a complex society. In addition, society is fluid, and so "sampling" it, no matter how carefully, is also illusory:

In human society, particularly in modern society, we are confronted with intricate complexes of moving relations which are roughly recognizable as systems, even though loose systems. Such a loose system is too complicated, too encumbered in detail and too fast moving to be described in any one of its given "cycles" of operation adequately and faithfully. . . . To know what is going on [with a national policy issue], particularly to know what is likely to go on in the latter stages, we have to dip in here and there. The problems of where to dip in, how to dip in, and how far to dip in [are of great concern].[12]

In the clash of opinions and groups, powerless and mighty, Blumer argues, we find the true texture of public opinion—the public opinion worth studying. Public opinion has a character and is tethered to a society in progress. As he puts it: "The formation of public opinion occurs as a function of a society in operation."[13]

Blumer's ideas were overrun in social science and largely ignored. The better survey researchers and pollsters acknowledge his contributions as an interesting challenge from the distant past, but Blumer certainly did not have the impact he had hoped he would have. Some in our day seem downright gleeful that, in midcentury, surveyors "won" in defining public opinion and Blumer lost.[14] Not a healthy or productive way to view critique by one of the most insightful scholars of the twentieth century, but the interest in legitimating surveying has been a steamroller of sorts. Many careers, institutes, academic departments, and companies are built upon survey methodology, and so the interest in protecting it naturally runs high. Surprisingly, not long after Blumer had been pronounced dead, the arrival of the Internet—the most important change in our communication environment since the introduction of television—leads us directly back to Blumer. I would argue that Blumer is more right than ever before: public opinion is most productively defined as a phenomenon in motion, replete with power dynamics, social stratification, and, most of all, conversation. If Blumer were alive today, he would view our blogs, Web pages, and constant chatter as extraordinarily helpful in understanding public opinion. In fact, it is precisely the sort of textured discourse that is so superior to the aggregation of anonymous individuals gathered in our artificial "publics" produced by polls. While we may worry about a tyranny of the majority—those who blog tend to get recognized—critics like Blumer see this as a natural sociological phenomenon in any period: from an empirical perspective, those who get heard typically have power already (through position, education, motivation, status), so their louder voice is simply a superstructural indicator of what lies beneath. To think anything else would, again, be ignoring fundamental social stratification already in existence.

The Internet Arrives

Polling has been a critical part of election campaigns and news reporting for many decades now, and those predicting election outcomes have done exceedingly well in calling the vote in U.S. presidential contests. Some of our pollsters miss it, but many are spot-on for the national vote numbers as well as the state figures. Those with a knowledge of poor predictions in the history of polling should be impressed with how far we've come and the sophistication so many of our survey researchers bring to the predictive task.

We love our polls and our horse race; preelection surveys will not disappear from campaigns any time soon. Far from it, we saw more polls than ever in the presidential campaign of 2008, and a variety of Web sites produced them for us on a daily basis. Some of these polls may have a dubious or mysterious methodology, some not, but we were flooded with numbers in 2008, and the demand for quantitative public opinion data to predict election outcomes seemed simply insatiable. It was hard to navigate the world last fall without noting the professional and amateur prediction attempts all around us; I was in a variety of restaurants that asked patrons to "cast their ballots" for Obama or McCain, and of course we did, tied up in the excitement of the race.[15]

This said, the definition of public opinion has actually become untethered from the polls predicting election outcomes. We are now settled with the notion that pollsters can predict who our next president will be, with fair accuracy. Some may complain about the horse race and criticize pollsters who miss the mark, but on the whole, we see that preelection polling by the better firms—close to Election Day—is reliable. What is not at all reliable or valid and has become practically irrelevant is issue polling.[16] We still read polls about issues—how Americans feel about abortion or foreign policy— but they seem suddenly irrelevant in a culture of talk and conversation. Put another way: our quantitative method of surveying predicts the quantitative outcome of elections beautifully, and that is as it should be. But the nature of public opinion *on issues* is now synonymous with talk and texture, not with quantitative data.

Examples abound, but some are simply astounding, given the young age of the Internet:

1. The explosion of blogs. We simply cannot count them—or settle on a number of blogs for very long. But it is clear that they grow in number and type on a daily basis as more people find their voice through the Internet. Citizens and leaders blog, but so do lobbyists and those working on behalf of our multinational corporations. Blogging is functional for many, impactful in many cases, and here to stay for a long while as an outlet for the expression of opinion across all content areas of the human experience.[17]

2. Mainstream attention to blogs. Bloggers do range from the proverbial "regular guy," blogging in his pajamas, to our highly sophisticated political observers like Andrew Sullivan (The Daily Dish). Somehow, taken collectively, they have become synonymous with public opinion in the eyes of our news organizations. Blog content is picked up and discussed on CNN, found in our most distinguished newspapers, and orients the talk of our statesmen, interest group leaders, college professors, and citizens. One channel on the XM satellite station— POTUS (Politics of the United States)—even has constant surveys of the blogs (its "blogcast") on the half hour, as if the blogs demand perpetual monitoring.

3. Twitter, Facebook, YouTube, and other sites as legitimate journalistic voices. It took many of us by surprise, but particularly during the unrest over the Iranian presidential elections of June 2009, due to the ban on foreign reporters, unconventional Internet outlets became critical in real reporting of the news. Mainstream broadcast and print media turned to blogs, but also to other, newer, often visual means of communication as legitimate partners in navigating newsworthy events. While this is largely a matter for journalists—how they do their work—media have always portrayed public opinion for their viewers and readers. So their techniques of reporting on public opinion also signal what journalists believe public opinion actually is.

These are only a few examples, but the point is that textured talk, dialogue, exchange, and conversation—not numbers—are the content of public opinion. With new venues for communication, we are no longer satisfied with statistics: they may be good for predicting election outcomes, but numbers do not quench our thirst for the feel and touch of American public opinion. In fact, the Internet—from truly ignorant chatter to incisive analysis—fills a gap we did not quite know existed. There has long been space for editorializing in newspapers and sparring of Sunday morning television pundits, but who knew that Americans would support such an expansive, varied, and intense mechanism for the expression of public opinion?[18] To compare the talk of the political Internet to the eighteenth-century salons is the best we can do in looking for a historical correlate to what we see now. Like the Internet talk, the political talk of salons could be brilliant, uneven, wild, and ridiculous all at once. But the conversation of the salons reflected and shaped the culture of France and much of Western Europe and ignited the revolutions that would change our world forever. We do not take the salons lightly now; they are invaluable to historians. And we should treat the Internet in precisely the same way.

If the salons and coffeehouses of the eighteenth century are the closest we have to historical correlates for the Internet, what can we learn from them about our own technology and our own times? They are difficult to compare due to the democracy that is Internet dialog relative to the elite nature of salons. And of course the salons were face-to-face gatherings, complete with friendship, flirtation, power dynamics, and all the other characteristics of interpersonal conversation. If there is one lesson to be learned, it is that talk is not—with all due respect to the economists—"cheap" in the least. Talk about politics, when it is intense, informed, and dominant, matters immensely. It finds its way into our most distinguished news venues and right on into the White House and Congress. Talk may seem like it leads nowhere directly, and that is often the case. But, as with the salons, we need to examine talk as an aggregate, for its direction and intensity, or we will simply be ignorant analysts of politics in our own time.

As I have discussed elsewhere, the eighteenth-century salon had some openness to the marginal actor: it was a place where a woman (albeit of a certain class) or a poor philosopher could get a hearing. Salons were not great social levelers (coffeehouses, with their low admission cost, were closer to this). But they did ignite and *enable* the unexpected line of thought, the provocative theory, and the serendipitous alliance. Perhaps this is what analysts of public opinion should be on alert for: not what a majority of bloggers think, since this is fluid and all bloggers are not alike or comparable. What we should focus on are the new ideas and the connections among social groups who communicate through the Internet. Network analysis of our Linked-In folks, our Twitterers, and others with Internet presence may reveal maps of the political future to come. And the ideas on the Internet are like a stream of political consciousness for an entire American policy, hard as this is to swallow for us old-fashioned social scientists.

I hate to speak authoritatively for the deceased, but I am nearly certain that Professor Blumer would find the political talk of the Internet far closer to "public opinion" than surveys. He would demand we develop theories, methods, and approaches that somehow capture the political content of the Internet. It is a daunting task, given the moving target the Internet has become—its international scope, dead links, lively sites, and general chaos. But he would be right to challenge us this way, and tools are beginning to appear to help us track the talk of the Internet. For example, Twitscoop is a site that—in real time—grabs keywords that are being used by greatest frequency by people who use Twitter. As the company explains on its Web site:

Twitscoop is a real-time visualization tool which enables users to "Mine the thought stream" provided by Twitter. Our algorithm cuts every English non-spam tweets into pieces ("tags"), and ranks them by how frequently they are used versus normal usage. Our web application detects growing trends in real-time, identifies breaking news (earthquakes, plane crashes, political events, new tech products etc.) and monitors specific keywords along with custom graphs that display the activity for any given word on twitter. Twitscoop can essentially be described as your real-time web's monitor.[19]

The techniques for tracking, aggregating, and analyzing talk are crude in 2010, but we will need to develop them as quickly as the commercial world does, driven by profit (in this case, attracting more people to Twitter). And at least in the case of Twitscoop, much of the talk is about celebrities or sporting events in progress. Nonetheless, one can imagine refining it and checking in while an important political event is in progress (e.g., a presidential debate).

One issue we need to struggle with, in tracking political conversation, is how much conversation out there is orchestrated. If a significant amount of content is manufactured by a political, corporate, or ideological organization, is it still talk that matters? This is a complex question and one that will demand focus on the individual case. But we will also need to be as attuned to the manufacture of conversation as we have been to the manufacture of polling numbers (produced by unqualified survey organizations or by innocent people just trying to show great numbers for their cause, even if the data are shaky).

The real question is whether we as scholars can keep up with all of this technological change, be open to new (and seemingly ancient yet relevant again) meanings of public opinion, or whether we will cling to the safety of our more conventional survey methods and aggregation-oriented meanings of knowing public opinion. I hope we can meet Blumer's high standards for honest empirical work and that the younger generation of public opinion researchers can blast the field open in ways that would make him proud.

NOTES

1. See Wilhelm Bauer, "Public Opinion," in *Encyclopaedia of the Social Sciences,* ed. E. Seligman, 669–74 (New York: Macmillan, 1930); Paul Lazarsfeld, "Public Opinion in the Classical Tradition," in *Qualitative Analysis: Historical and Critical Essays,* 300–317 (Boston: Allyn and Bacon, 1972); and Jurgen Habermas, *The Structural Transformation of the Public Sphere: An Inquiry into a Category of Bourgeois Society* (Cambridge, MA: MIT Press, 1989).

2. Paul Palmer, "The Concept of Public Opinion in Political Theory," in *Essays in History and Political Theory in Honor of Charles Howard McIlwain,* ed. C. Wittke, 230–57 (New York: Russell and Russell, 1936).

3. Ibid., 239.

4. On the salons, please see my *Politics at the Margin: Historical Studies of Public Expression outside the Mainstream* (New York: Cambridge University Press, 1994).

5. Ibid., chap. 3.

6. Patricia Cline Cohen, *A Calculating People: The Spread of Numeracy in Early America* (Chicago: University of Chicago Press, 1983).

7. See my *Numbered Voices: How Opinion Polls Have Shaped American Politics* (Chicago:

University of Chicago Press, 1993). In this book, I explore the tensions between our desire for representation of the public (through the survey sample) and the texture of public opinion.

8. A. N. Holcombe, "The Measurement of Public Opinion," *American Political Science Review* 19 (February 1925): 123–26.

9. Ibid, 123–24.

10. Lindsay Rogers, *The Pollsters: Public Opinion, Politics, and Democratic Leadership* (New York: Knopf, 1949), 17; Amy Fried, "The Forgotten Lindsay Rogers and the Development of American Political Science," *American Political Science Review* 100 (2006): 555–61.

11. Herbert Blumer, "Public Opinion and Public Opinion Polling," *American Sociological Review* 13 (1948): 242–49.

12. Ibid., 549.

13. Ibid, 544.

14. See Philip Converse, "Changing Conceptions of Public Opinion in the Political Process," *Public Opinion Quarterly* 51, Supplement (1987): 12–24.

15. Two popular polling Web sites during the 2008 campaign that offered numerous polls and analysis were pollster.com and realclearpolitics.com.

16. Issue polling can be excellent and thoughtful, as in the surveys presented by the Pew Foundation, academic organizations, and others. But the vast majority of issue polls are quickly done and not particularly well executed. We see these daily on television broadcasts and in our newspapers and Web sites. With regard to the problems and challenges of issue polling and attitude surveying more generally, there are a variety of journals, books, and organizations devoted to these matters. The premier organization in this area is the American Association for Public Opinion Research, which publishes the *Public Opinion Quarterly.* For a sophisticated look at the comprehensive challenges of surveying on the issues, see Robert M. Groves, F. J. Fowler, Mick P. Couper, James M. Lepkowski, Eleanor Singer, and R. Tourangeau, *Survey Methodology* (New York: Wiley, 2004).

17. We see an increasing number of Web sites devoted to locating and analyzing blogs. One serious attempt is www.technoratimedia.com.

18. One answer might be Alexis De Tocqueville, who commented that "an American cannot converse, but he can discuss, and his talk falls into a dissertation." It is questionable, however, whether Tocqueville's observation provides an appropriate analogy to Internet talk. That conversation is also beyond the scope of this chapter. See Alexis De Tocqueville, *Democracy in America* (New York: Century Co., 1893), 319.

19. See: www.twitscoop.com/about/.

6

Too Much Talk, Not Enough Action?
Political Expression in a Digital Age

KIRBY GOIDEL, ASHLEY KIRZINGER, AND MICHAEL XENOS

In contemporary politics, individual citizens have more opportunities than ever before to express political opinions across a wider range of venues. For many observers, this has all the making of a democratic resurgence. The democratic dialogue is more open and free flowing, and political movements can emerge from the ground up in ways unimaginable just ten years ago. Operating independently of political campaigns, individual citizens can post videos on YouTube, comment on news stories, create and maintain political blogs, or organize Facebook friends into political action. Operating in coordination with political parties, campaigns, or interest groups, individuals can amplify their collective voice and affect policy decisions and debates.

In this chapter, we explore how these increased opportunities for political expression affect our understanding of public opinion. Specifically, we seek to answer two questions. First, does the online expression of political opinions provide a useful indicator of public opinion, or has it simply added noise to the policy-making process? From a measurement standpoint, the expression of unfiltered opinions provides public opinion scholars with a unique opportunity—an almost unlimited supply of public commentary on politically and socially relevant issues. But does such commentary illuminate discussions or distort efforts to accurately gauge public sentiments? If we take V. O.

Key's definition of public opinion as "those opinions held by private persons which governments find it prudent to heed," one can reasonably question whether online opinion expression has taken on greater political and social significance than public opinion polling particularly as political campaigns emphasize mobilizing the base rather than attracting the median voter.[1]

Second, has the online expression of political opinions fundamentally altered the structure of public opinion? We take as a starting point Susan Herbst's useful distinction in Chapter 5 between public opinion as conversation (or talk) and public opinion as counting. Online news sources provide the potential for a more informed citizenry, and online opinion forums (e.g., blogs, discussion groups, news commentary) provide the potential for a more deliberative and thoughtful public. Has this potential been realized? Or, to borrow a phrase from Neil Postman, are we simply "amusing ourselves to death," so diverted by entertainment choices that we no longer pay adequate attention to civic and political content?[2] In answering the first question, we seek to understand whether the increased avenues available for political expression improve our measurement of public opinion. In answering the second, we seek to understand whether online political expression has fundamentally altered the nature of what we are attempting to measure.

Political Expression as an Indicator of Public Opinion

Imagine if we could somehow capture the universe of political talk around any given political issue. This would include all the statements one might make to others (friends, family, and co-workers) and would include the various modes of opinion expression (face to face, e-mail, and online commentary). If we could capture this universe, sample from it, and develop appropriate measures of the content, would it provide a richer and deeper understanding of public opinion than can be derived from even the most carefully constructed and well-executed opinion polls? Arguably, such a scenario would provide a better understanding of public opinion, as we would be able to detect the direction of opinion, its intensity, and how it is expressed in naturally occurring contexts.

Now imagine that we can capture only a limited range of political talk—opinions expressed online via relatively public venues—missing the private and personal interactions that make up the vast majority of political conversation. Does online political talk provide a useful indicator of public opinion? Or is it simply noise distorting representative public opinion by amplifying the voice of the most intensely partisan and ideologically motivated citizens?

To answer these questions, it is important to distinguish who is talking online. We can begin by thinking of opinion expression as a rational form of political participation in which individuals express opinions when the benefits of doing so outweigh any associated costs. In a digital age, the opportunities for opinion expression are virtually unlimited, providing politically motivated citizens with a multitude of forums and formats. Equally important, once one is connected to the Internet (an important consideration we will return to later), there are little or no hard costs associated with expressing an opinion. Online opinion expression is virtually cost-free, particularly when compared with more traditional forms of political activity that require being physically in a specific place at a specific time—for example, voting, attending meetings, or volunteering for political campaigns. To the extent that opinions are expressed within relatively friendly forums, the social costs associated with expressing an unpopular opinion are also minimized. There is no spiral of silence on the Internet, as virtually every opinion can find a relatively friendly audience to confirm and reinforce existing beliefs.[3]

Despite the low costs, political expression through online forums is not a particularly common activity and appears to be directed primarily at existing social and political networks. In Table 6.1, we present the percentage of adults who reported engaging in various forms of online political communication. Twenty-eight percent of adults communicated with others about politics using the Internet during the 2008 presidential elections, but fewer than one in ten posted a comment in a publicly accessible venue. When comments are posted, they are most commonly posted on social networking sites that limit access to identified "friends" rather than on news sites or political blogs. We do not want to overstate the point: political communication is undoubtedly facilitated by digital media, but it is most often occurring within the relatively friendly confines of existing networks—for example, a co-worker sending political commentary he or she agrees with or finds amusing. The important difference is that a single individual can reach

Table 6.1.

Online Political Expression among Adults and Young Adults

	All Adults (%)	Young Adults (%)
Communication with others about politics, the campaign, or the 2008 elections using the Internet	27.9	38.2
Send or receive e-mail	32.5	40.8
Send or receive text	14.0	29.1
Use instant messaging to talk about politics	9.5	21.7
Use Twitter to post thoughts or experiences	1.3	2.9
Contribute money online	6.3	7.1
Sign up to volunteer	4.5	7.4
Share audio, photos, or video files related to the campaign	12.4	17.9
Forward someone else's political commentary or writing	20.5	24.9
Forward someone else's audio or video	14.0	18.0
Customize Web page to display new political or campaign information	3.5	6.4
Posted comments in online discussion	5.8	9.9
Posted comments on a blog	6.0	10.1
Posted comments on social networking site	7.6	18.9
Posted comments on any Web site	6.7	9.5
Started or joined a political group on a social networking site	4.3	10.3
Signed up as a "friend" of a candidate on a social networking site	3.3	8.3

Source: Pew Internet, November 2008, Post Election Survey.

hundreds or thousands of "friends" and family through e-mail, tweets, and Facebook postings, far more than would be possible through face-to-face communication. This networked information economy provides a nonmarket alternative to traditional news sources allowing individual users to drive the political conversation based on what they find interesting and engaging rather than the more controlled mass media model of the broadcast era.[4]

Along these lines, Table 6.1 also demonstrates that respondents were more likely to forward someone else's writings than to post original commentary. Twenty-one percent of adults forwarded someone else's political commentary, while only 6 percent posted comments on a political blog or online discussion. Political communication may be facilitated by online media, but it is often the recycling of material by means of forwarded e-mail messages and YouTube videos. While these trends are somewhat consistent with a classic two-step flow reading of opinion formation and online expression, it is difficult to overlook the relatively low frequency of expression overall in these data.

To place the patterns in Table 6.1 in context, we can contrast online communication with more traditional indicators of political involvement as reflected in the American National Election Studies. In 2004, ANES reported that 48 percent of respondents tried to persuade someone to vote for or against one of the presidential candidates, 7 percent attended a political meeting, 3 percent worked for a party or campaign, and 13 percent contributed money online. We should note a caveat here, as online communication may be expressed to a more diverse set of social networks and, consequently, online discussants may be more likely to express opposing political views.

If there is a silver lining, it is that young people (ages 18–34) are more likely to use digital media to engage in political talk. With the notable exception of age, however, online political participation suffers from the same socioeconomic and partisan biases that underlie other forms of engagement. While access to Internet has increased, many Internet users cannot complete simple online tasks, much less contribute to online blogs or message boards. It appears that Internet efficacy falls down across similar socioeconomic lines leading to what scholars refer to as a second-level digital divide.[5] The lack of Internet knowledge further hinders access to participation. Moreover, research has similarly found that higher-status Internet users are more likely to use the Internet for "capital-enhancing activities," thus increasing the knowledge gap.[6]

This pattern of participation, referred to as the digital divide, remains an important component of new media use, though recent research has emphasized differences in use across levels of political engagement.[7] For example, in Table 6.2 we present a logistic regression estimating the individual probability that a respondent communicated with others using the Internet

Table 6.2.

Logistic Regression of Online Communication on Demographics and Partisan Intensity

Variables	Coefficients (Standard errors)
Education	.368*
	(.042)
Age	−.024*
	(.003)
Income	.143*
	(.029)
Race (1 = nonwhite)	.043
	(.163)
Sex (1 = female)	.167
	(.118)
Partisan intensity	.334*
	(.095)
Party affiliation (Democratic = high)	.012
	(.035)
Constant	−3.22
	(.408)
Pseudo R-square	.126

Source: Pew Internet, November 2008, Post Election Survey.

Note: The dependent variables is coded 1 if the respondent reported communicating with the others about politics, the campaign, or the 2008 elections using the Internet, 0 otherwise. * $p < .05$.

during the 2008 elections. Logistic regression tells us whether individuals with specific characteristics (e.g., education and partisan intensity) are more likely to communicate about politics using the Internet. The results displayed in Table 6.2 indicate that online political communication is a function of education, age, income, race, sex, partisan intensity, and partisan affiliation.

To better illustrate the results, we computed the probability of communicating online by partisan intensity and education. This is displayed in Figure 6.1. As can be seen in the figure, political independents were about

Figure 6.1. Probability of Communicating about Politics Online

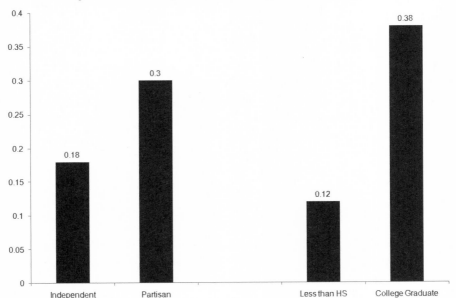

half as likely as partisan to communicate about politics online. The effects are even more pronounced for education. A college graduate is three times more like to participate than someone without a college degree. The result is that online political talk is polarized, with highly educated and ideologically driven Democrats and Republicans, liberals and conservatives, talking more loudly and more often. As with other forms of participation, lower-income, less educated, and less partisan citizens are left out of the conversation.

Overall, online political talk may open up avenues of political communication, but it suffers from the same socioeconomic and self-selection biases that infected efforts to gauge public sentiments prior to the development of the modern public opinion poll. Just as one cannot infer public sentiments from letters to the editor or callers to talk radio shows, online political expression is far too limited to reflect public sentiments. If the voices of the less involved, less educated, and less partisan are important, the "radical" equality of the public opinion poll remains the best mechanism for gauging public opinion, even as conversation-based public opinion blossoms within cyberspace.

In one respect, however, online political talk may prove to be more useful than traditional approaches to measuring public opinion. To the extent that American politics is best characterized as pluralist—rather than majoritarian—democracy, online political talk can help us better illuminate whose voice government is heeding. When it comes to news coverage of political issues, for example, online political talk may also provide contextual understanding of the agenda-setting process and framing contests, illuminating which voices are most influential in setting the public agenda and defining the frames through which public issues are constructed.[8] In an increasing polarized political environment, this is no small accomplishment, but it falls short of representative opinion.

Digital Media and the Structure of Public Opinion

If online political talk has limited value as a substitute for measuring public opinion, has it transformed the structure of public opinion in important ways? In this section, we consider two possibilities. First, by providing a wider range of information sources and making these sources more readily available, the Internet may lead to a more informed public. Second, by expanding the conversation online, the process by which the public comes to judgment on public issues may be structured differently and perhaps may even be more deliberative.

To begin, there can be little question as to the growing importance of online news sources. As newspaper readership has declined and television news audiences have dwindled, the percentage of Americans turning to online news sources has consistently increased. According to the Pew Center, the percentage of adults who "got news online yesterday" increased from 22 percent in March 2000 to 38 percent in April 2009. Similarly, the percentage saying they ever look for news about politics or upcoming campaigns online increased from 35 to 60 percent over the same period.[9] Increasingly when citizens need information, they are going online to get it.

Studies consistently find that individuals who get their political news online are significantly more knowledgeable about politics. However, this increase in knowledge comes with an expanding "knowledge gap" between the politically engaged and the politically disinterested.[10] The key variable appears to be the motivation to seek out political content. In this respect, expanded choice in information allows interested individuals to gain appreciably more knowledge about the political process, but it also allows the disinterested to avoid politics altogether.[11] More media choices have, perhaps ironically, decreased both political involvement and political knowledge. No longer do people receive a daily source of political news while watching their evening television news, described by Markus Prior as by-product learning. As the media environment becomes more efficient, people who are more likely to watch entertainment shows are less likely to learn political information because they encounter it less frequently.[12] This allows individual news consumption to be highly economical, but it also means that individuals encounter fewer opportunities for learning. While the availability of political information has drastically increased online, the number of those who access it has decreased. Heavy online use does not translate to higher levels of political knowledge. In a study of Louisiana adults, for example, frequency of social networking use was associated with lower levels of political knowledge.[13]

Expanded choice also allows individuals to seek out ideologically comforting news sources that confirm rather than challenge preexisting beliefs. The carefully constructed niche marketing of Fox News as the "fair and balanced" alternative to liberal news networks is only the most obvious example. Increasingly liberals and conservatives alike turn to information sources that share their ideological predispositions. The result is an increasing polarized news audience.[14]

The fault appears to reside less in the medium than in human nature. While a considerable amount of work in political science and economics assumes rational political actors, we know that human beings succumb to various psychological processes that make everyday interactions fall far short of rational expectations. Given an expanded and increasingly diverse information environment, we might hope citizens would purposefully sample some of the available sources to ensure they understand competing perspectives or to expose themselves to alternative views. However, as is well established in information-processing literature, human beings are far more likely to be cognitive misers than Baysian statisticians when it comes to selecting, attending to, and retaining political information.

Perhaps ironically, the number of sources may reinforce rather than challenge this fundamental instinct. As individuals become overwhelmed with information, they may be more inclined to seek trusted and more entertaining sources—Rush Limbaugh, Jon Stewart, or favored bloggers—to help cut through the clutter and quickly make sense of a complex and confusing world. The economics of a digital media environment may reinforce this as news and entertainment sources seek to carve out an identifiable niche of readers or viewers.[15] In the age of broadcast news, networks competed for the equivalent of the median voter—or average viewer—and, in doing so, sought to avoid overt political bias. News coverage in such an information environment was necessarily directed toward the mainstream of American politics. The digital age fundamentally alters this calculus. Fox News, for example, does not need to appeal to the average viewer but can instead appeal directly to self-identified conservative viewers.[16] The unanswered question is what happens to moderate voters and independents in an age of increasing polarized news?

Cass Sunstein makes a similar point in his discussion of enclave deliberations. According to Sunstein, today's media environment is overloaded with "too many options, too many topics, too many opinions." Those seeking online political information retreat into "echo chambers of their own design" and are subsequently walled off from diverse viewpoints and new ideas.[17] The result is a cluster of polarized groups with few common reference points. While Sunstein may be too pessimistic in his view of online political talk, his point is clear: the online political sphere does not encourage or facilitate crosscutting political talk.

The big picture is this: an expanding information environment does not lead to a more informed citizenry. Some citizens will be more informed, but others will avoid political news and information altogether. The more compelling story involves the further fragmentation and segmentation of the audience. This includes the movement to partisan news sources and the movement away from news altogether. In many ways, this is a step backward as selectivity biases and opinion leaders play an increased role in the interpretation of news stories and events. What is more difficult to discern is the degree to which citizens are learning online through incidental exposure to online political content in a manner akin to soft news exposure.[18]

The Prospects for Online Deliberation

One of the most enduring and troubling critiques of public opinion polling is that it presents contrived on-the-spot survey responses as socially relevant and political meaningful public opinion. Even when survey questions pertain to topics on which respondents likely have little information or considerable ambivalence, critics contend, survey results are presented as though they reflect public preferences.[19] Nuanced interpretations of survey results can capture this ambivalence, but such nuance is too often absent from media coverage of poll results.

Proponents of deliberative opinion polling subsequently contend that meaningful public opinion emerges only after a deliberative process in which the public carefully considers competing perspectives and weighs policy alternatives.[20] The role of a deliberative democracy, as defined by Amy Gutmann and Dennis Thompson, is to "affirm the need to justify decisions made by citizens and their representatives."[21] While there are many versions of what deliberation looks like, John Gastil provides an unassailable definition of what it truly means when people deliberate: "They carefully examine a problem and arrive at a well-reasoned solution after a period of inclusive, respectful consideration of diverse points of view."[22] According to extant research, at least in some settings group discussion can meet the expectations of deliberative theorists.[23] Deliberation can also occur online. If democracy entails equal opportunity to participate in politics, then the Internet creates that opportunity. The greatest hope of technological enthusiasts is that the online media would provide a forum for meaningful deliberation. Does online opinion expression provide for a more deliberative public opinion?

For reasons noted earlier, the answer appears to be no. Opening up the number of venues for public participation appears to attract the intensely partisan more interested in promoting a particular view than in hearing from the other side. In an excellent and comprehensive exploration of exposure to political talk in interpersonal settings, Diana Mutz concludes that hearing competing perspectives increases tolerance and understanding but decreases political involvement. As Mutz concludes, the political implications are quite profound: we can have a participatory democracy or a deliberative democracy but not both.[24] A more polarized electorate may be more engaged but not necessarily more informed, deliberative, or thoughtful. The upshot is that polarization may increase participation particularly among the base.

The caveat added by online political expression is that, to the extent that entertainment options are available, increases in involvement among partisans may not translate into increases in aggregate participation rates or increased political knowledge. In a 2009 study of Louisiana adults, for example, we found that time spent on social networking sites such as Facebook was negatively associated with neutral political knowledge.[25] In a 2009 study of online political discussion, Magdalena Wojcieszak and Diana Mutz similarly report that exposure to opposing political views tends to occur primarily in online forums where politics is incidental (and not central) to the conversation.[26] Other research has found that online deliberation is less likely to result in consensus than are face-to-face deliberations.[27]

Even so, it is no doubt important for public opinion scholars to recognize the vast power that online political talk holds for both opinion expression and the measurement of public opinion. But as Benjamin Barber argued in 1998, the Internet's real tragedy was that it had not provided a public place or civic space for public deliberation. "In moments of national gravity or national tragedy—the assassination of a President, a terrorist incident, the end of a war," Barber wrote, "we need common places to gather and common turf on which to grieve or celebrate."[28] So while new technological and communication systems can offer a platform for the public sphere, what is also needed is the ability to sift through all the variations of opinions and attitudes held by individuals. Or in Yochai Benkler's words, "Render them in ways that make them sufficiently salient in the overall mix of potential opinions to form a condensation point for collective action."[29] To date, the deliberative potential of the Internet remains mostly unrealized.

Conclusions

While we can celebrate the democratic potential of new media, the reality falls far short of this promise. Although there are more avenues to express political opinions and engage in political dialogue than ever before, participation remains the province of the most interested and motivated. And even though the sources of political information have grown and diversified, individual citizens have responded by seeking information sources that share their personal predispositions and biases. News and information sources are increasingly cast in the partisan hues.

As with so much of the work on public opinion, however, we may simply expect too much from the average citizen. The average citizen with a full-time job, family, and other interests is unlikely to expose him- or herself to a diversity of political views. Average citizens lack the time, interest, and resources. Instead, they need to find trusted opinion leaders to help make sense of the political world. Seen in this light, the most powerful potential of new media—only partially realized during the Obama campaign—is the capacity it provides elites to efficiently mobilize and engage political supporters. Social networking sites, text messaging, Twitter, and other readily accessible information tools allow elites to share real-time information, collect data on supporters, and put out calls for political action.

Because of the wealth of data that can be collected, a call to action or specific issue appeal can be carefully tailored to match the interests and concerns of the individual supporter. In return, supporters can offer feedback, giving them a sense of ownership in the campaign. Seen in this light, new media have the potential to reinvigorate democratic governance, but it is a much different model than often imagined—not more deliberative or more informed but collective action mobilized by political parties, candidates, and interest groups.

This reality returns us to a central point of this volume: democracy needs credible public opinion polling. Well-constructed polls force policymakers to hear the voices in the middle—the less partisan and the less engaged—voices notably missing from other channels of political engagement. By providing greater opportunities for expression, the Internet has proven to be a boon to intense partisans and committed ideologues but a bust for less committed and less ideological citizens. More to the point, neither the remarkable expansion of political expression made possible by digital media nor the shortcomings of contemporary polling change this central fact: public opinion polls capture a wider range of opinion than any other form of political expression. In doing so, polling helps to move politics away from the extremes and toward the center. As George Gallup wrote in 1957:

I am firmly convinced that if, during the last twenty years, public opinion had manifested itself only by letters to congressmen, the lobbying of pressure groups, and the reports of political henchmen—as it did prior to the advent of the sample polls—the country would have almost certainly been lead in the wrong direction at several points.[30]

This is not to discount the value of deliberation. Deliberative processes can help inform moderate voters attracted to conversations that acknowledge competing perspectives and policy alternatives.[31] Deliberation, however, is unlikely to occur naturally in the current information environment. Online opinion expression is self-selected and highly partisan. Mere exposure to competing views is rare. And online conversations seldom move toward consensus or shared understanding. Absent meaningful deliberation, public opinion polling can serve as moderating force in an increasingly polarized environment.

NOTES

1. V. O. Key Jr., *Public Opinion and American Democracy* (New York: Knopf, 1961), 14.

2. Neil Postman, *Amusing Ourselves to Death: Public Discourse in an Age of Show Business* (New York: Viking, 1985).

3. Ho and McLeod contend that the absence of social pressures means computer-mediated discussion more closely approximates deliberation than does face-to-face communication; see Shirley Ho and Douglas McLeod, "Social-Psychological Influences on Expression in Face-to-Face and Computer-Mediated Communication," *Communication Research* 35 (2008): 190–207.

4. Yochai Benkler, *The Wealth of Networks: How Social Production Transforms Markets and Freedom* (New Haven: Yale University Press, 2006).

5. Eszter Hargittai, "Second-Level Digital Divide: Differences in People's Online Skills," *First Monday* 7 (2002). www.firstmonday.org/htbin/cgiwrap/bin/ojs/index.php/fm/article/viewArticle/942/864 (accessed April 10, 2010).

6. Nicole Zillien and Eszter Haggattai, "Digital Distinctions: Status-Specific Types of Internet Usage," *Social Science Quarterly* 90 (2009): 270–91.

7. For a complete literature review on how the digital divide affects online participation, see Michael Margolis and David Resnick, *Politics as Usual: The Cyberspace "Revolution"* (Thousand Oaks, CA: Sage Publications, 2000), and Pippa Norris, *Digital Divide: Civic Engagement, Information Poverty, and the Internet Worldwide* (Cambridge: Cambridge University Press, 2001).

8. W. Lance Bennett and Shanto Iyengar, "A New Era of Minimal Effects? The Changing Foundations of Political Communication," *Journal of Communication* 58 (2008): 707–31.

9. Data from 2009 are taken from the Pew Internet & American Life Project. Methodology: Interviewing conducted by Princeton Survey Research Associates International, March 26–April 19, 2009, and based on 2,253 telephone interviews. Sample: national adult; 1,162 respondents were interviewed on a landline telephone, and 561 were interviewed on a cell phone. Data from 2000 are taken from the Pew Internet & American Life Project. Methodology: Interviewing conducted by Princeton Survey Research Associates, March 1–March 31, 2000, and based

on 3,533 telephone interviews. Retrieved July 22, 2010, from the iPOLL Databank, The Roper Center for Public Opinion Research, University of Connecticut, www.ropercenter.uconn.edu/data_access/ipoll/ipoll.html.

10. Phillip J. Tichenor, George A. Donohue, and Clarice Olien, "Mass Media Flow and Differential Growth in Knowledge," *Public Opinion Quarterly* 34 (1970): 159–70.

11. Bennett and Iyengar, "New Era of Minimal Effects?"; Markus Prior, "News vs. Entertainment: How Increasing Media Choice Widens Gaps in Political Knowledge and Turnout," *American Journal of Political Science* 49 (2005): 577–92.

12. Markus Prior, *Post-Broadcast Democracy: How Media Choice Increases Inequality in Political Involvement and Polarizes Elections* (New York: Cambridge University Press, 2007).

13. R. Kirby Goidel, Christopher Kenny, and Michael Xenos, "New Media Use, Political Sophistication, and Cell Phone Surveys" (paper presented at the American Association of Public Opinion Research, Hollywood, FL, May 14–17, 2009).

14. Barry Hollander, "Tuning Out or Tuning Elsewhere? Partisanship, Polarization, and Media Migration from 1998 to 2006," *Journalism and Mass Communication Quarterly* 85 (2008): 23–40; Shanto Iyengar and Kyu Hahn, "Red Media, Blue Media: Evidence of Ideological Selectivity in Media Use," *Journal of Communication* 59 (2009): 19–39; Natalie Stroud, "Media Use and Political Predispositions: Revisiting the Concept of Selective Exposure," *Political Behavior* 30 (2008): 341–66.

15. James Hamilton, *All the News That's Fit to Sell: How the Market Transforms Information into News* (Princeton: Princeton University Press, 2004).

16. Bennett and Iyengar, "New Era of Minimal Effects?"

17. Cass Sunstein, *Republic.com* (Princeton: Princeton University Press, 2001).

18. Matthew Baum, *Soft News Goes to War: Public Opinion and American Foreign Policy in the New Media Age* (Princeton: Princeton University Press, 2003).

19. David Moore, *The Opinion Makers: An Insider Exposes the Truth behind the Polls* (Boston: Beacon Press, 2008).

20. Bruce Ackerman and James Fishkin, *Deliberation Day* (New Haven: Yale University Press, 2004); James Fishkin, *Democracy and Deliberation: New Directions for Democratic Reform* (New Haven: Yale University Press, 1991).

21. Amy Gutmann and Dennis Thompson, *Why Deliberative Democracy?* (Princeton: Princeton University Press, 2004).

22. John Gastil, *Political Communication and Deliberation* (Thousand Oaks, CA: Sage, 2008).

23. Tali Mendelberg, "The Deliberative Citizen: Theory and Evidence," in *Research in Micropolitics,* vol. 6: *Political Decision Making, Deliberation and Participation,* ed. Michael X. Delli Carpini, Leonie Huddy, and Robert Shapiro, 151–193 (Greenwich, CT: JAI Press, 2002).

24. Diana Mutz, *Hearing the Other Side: Deliberative versus Participatory Democracy* (Cambridge: Cambridge University Press, 2006).

25. Goidel, Kenny, and Xenos, "New Media Use, Political Sophistication, and Cell Phone Surveys."

26. Magdalena Wojcieszak and Diana Mutz, "Online Groups and Political Discourse: Do

Online Discussion Spaces Facilitate Exposure to Political Disagreement?" *Journal of Communication* 59 (2009): 40–56.

27. Young Min Baek, Magdalena Wojcieszak, and Michael X. Delli Carpini, "Online versus Face-to-Face Deliberation: Who? Why? What? With What Effects?" (paper presented at the annual meeting of the American Political Science Association, Boston, MA, August 28, 2008).

28. Benjamin Barber, "Which Technology and Which Democracy," *MIT Communications Forum,* December 6, 1998, www.web.mit.edu/comm-forum/papers/barber.html (accessed April 10, 2010).

29. Benkler, *Wealth of Networks.*

30. George Gallup, "The Changing Climate for Public Opinion Research," *Public Opinion Quarterly* 21 (1957): 23–27.

31. R. Kirby Goidel, Craig Freeman, Steven Procopio, and Charles Zewe, "Who Participates in the 'Public Square' and Does It Matter?" *Public Opinion Quarterly* 72 (2008): 792–803.

7

Alternatives to Polling

ANNA GREENBERG

I enter this conversation about the future of public opinion polling with academic training in survey research methodology but also largely as a practitioner, or a "pollster." My clients are candidates running for office as well as advocacy groups, whose primary interest in public opinion lies in its role as a tool to help them win elections or influence public policy. They place a high premium on the accuracy of their polls but also on the ways that public opinion research can be used to inform decisions about strategy, including messaging and targeting. Changes in communications technologies and the rise of new media pose real challenges to our ability to provide accurate and actionable information to our clients but also create opportunities for new ways to gather data to inform strategy, particularly message testing and voter targeting.

Traditionally, political polling firms rely primarily on surveys conducted over landlines either using random digit dial (RDD) methodology or using samples pulled from state voter files. These two methods continue to be the gold standard for accurate political polling, with all the caveats about response rates and nonresponse bias, and the primary tool for political and advocacy campaigns. As Charles Franklin noted in his presentation at the 2009 Breaux Symposium, these surveys continue to be accurate even as they underrepresent certain demographic groups or certain kinds of voters. It is hard, in the near term, to imagine campaigns moving away from this approach, as they need to understand who is winning and losing and the best path toward winning elections and policy battles.[1]

But as Robert Goidel and Scott Keeter both point out, changes in communications technology and the rise of new media have created both short-term and long-term challenges to our ability to conduct accurate survey research. An increasing number of people—particularly younger people and people of color—are simply not available to participate in surveys over a landline. In the short term, while cell phone sampling is possible and increasingly incorporated into survey research, it is significantly more expensive than landline interviewing and out of reach for most political clients. In the long term, it is hard to see how any political or advocacy campaign will be able to avoid interviewing on cell phones or through other means (e.g., text messaging) as Generation Y becomes an increasingly larger part of the overall electorate. In other words, research for political and advocacy campaigns must move to multimode approaches if it is going to capture the real universe of voters.

Equally as important, the country is changing in ways that challenge a model of public opinion that simply relies on the aggregation of individual "opinions" gathered over a telephone. Standardized phone surveys assume that people have the same information about issues or think about issues in the same ways, which may have been *truer* in recent years (a dubious assumption in and of itself) when political communication was dominated by broadcast news and newspapers. Now, if people are interested in politics, they can cull their own information—especially online—or they are as likely to receive information peer to peer through such avenues as forwarded e-mails as they are in the newspaper. Moreover, discussion groups and blogs provide a forum for people to engage in a real discussion about the issues of the day. Of course, as Susan Herbst notes in her essay, this "dialogic" aspect of public opinion, albeit electronic, is nothing new; we are just rediscovering it. Simply put, a "top-down" traditional approach to public opinion research does not account for the more organic, bottom-up way opinion forms and ultimately shapes broader attitudes.[2]

Luckily, new technologies allow us to overcome some of the inherent limitations of traditional landline-based survey research. These technologies not only open up avenues for reaching populations underrepresented in traditional research (e.g., younger people) but also help us use creative methods to tap into the kind of political information people receive and process. Moreover, these new technologies allow us to be more creative in how we measure opinion, not just gauging reactions to questions written by pollsters but allowing respondents to drive content, and ultimately how we ask questions themselves.

Equally important, these new approaches focus less on prediction or accuracy and more on understanding trends, relationships, and language. They help us paint a richer portrait of public opinion; from a political strategic perspective, these approaches allow us to get closer to determining what moves people in the real world, as opposed to in the course of hearing a survey over the phone or sitting around with people in a focus group.

Some of these new technologies also have the benefit of making some research more affordable. As response rates decline, it has become increasingly expensive to conduct RDD, landline surveys with live interviewers; maintaining a representative sample requires longer fielding windows and more callbacks, which means higher calling costs. Web-based research and interactive voice recognition (IVR) do not require live interviewers, and the main cost associated with these surveys is purchasing sample and programming time. Of course, not all the new technologies reduce survey costs; cell phone interviewing can cost three times as much as a live landline interview.

This chapter looks at ways political polling firms are expanding how they measure public opinion, focusing on the rise of Web-based research, micro-targeting and data mining, and experimentation. These approaches are only in the beginning stages of integration into the work of polling firms because they are still developing as strategic tools for campaigns and because campaigns have limited research budgets. These methods by no means account for a substantial portion of political polling firms' revenue but are increasingly offered as part of a package of research tools to clients.

Web-Based Public Opinion Research

It is easy to focus on the problems of Web-based public opinion research rather than the creative opportunities it creates. Initially, the main concern about Web-based research was that samples are drawn from panels of self-selected respondents who have both access to the Internet and an interest in taking surveys. Near-universal access to the Internet alleviated some of these concerns, though most Web-based research is still based primarily on nonrandom samples.[3] The proliferation of polls in the media stems, in part, from the relatively low cost of conducting Web-based research. These surveys have real problems with accuracy that no amount of weighting can fix, and campaigns shy away from giving them too much credence, though they often drive press coverage with which campaigns must contend. But these legitimate concerns about the samples used for Web-based research threaten to diminish some of the real innovation and learning that can take place with this kind of research.[4]

First, we can reach special populations that would be prohibitively expensive or even impossible to reach over the phone. We now have the ability to conduct surveys among groups like Jewish Americans, young people, people with particular medical conditions, female business owners, and the like at a reasonable cost. Certainly, this research will have all the limitations of nonrepresentative, nonrandom samples, but in most cases some reasonably reliable information is better than no information at all.

Second, Web-based research changes how we collect public opinion data. While we are still reaching respondents from the top down in the sense that we are inviting them to participate in research, the Web format allows respondents to drive content. Open-ended questions allow respondents to tell us what they think the country's biggest problems are or what President Obama should do about health care reform. We can collect much more extensive and richly written responses, with the exact language respondents use, than an interviewer captures on the phone. Web-based research also allows us to capture trends in public opinion that are coming from the bottom up. For example, during the 2008 presidential election, our online open-ended tracking captured voters' doubts about Sarah Palin before tracking surveys and the media coverage noted her declining poll numbers.

Third, the Web-based format allows more creative data collection. The visual format allows respondents to react to the spoken word delivered by different kinds of messengers. Reading a message paragraph over the phone or in a focus group does not capture the emotion or connection that different kinds of messengers convey. For candidates, in particular, understanding how voters react to what they see and hear from candidates can provide invaluable information. In the past, this kind of research was pretty typical for a presidential candidate or a well-funded statewide race, but the affordability of Web-based research opens this research to campaigns at every level. Here again, we can gauge reactions in an open-ended written format or use virtual "dial meters" to measure the emotions and reactions of respondents to certain images, as well as substantive content.

The written format of Web-based research allows respondents to deconstruct messages instead of just testing reactions to long, complex statements on the phone. There is a move to do more in-depth "narrative" testing online in both its written and visual format. Respondents can react to language, phrases, and emotions instead of just rating whether a statement makes them more or less likely to support a candidate.

Finally, Web-based research allows for inexpensive, large-scale experimentation, particularly in the testing of advertisements and print campaign materials. In the past, political and advocacy campaigns tested their ads in focus groups (to the extent that they were tested at all). In these groups, ten people sit around a table to watch, evaluate, and discuss an ad, yielding rich qualitative information but in no way replicating the real environment in which voters see political advertising. Web-based research allows pollsters to test an almost unlimited number of ads—as long as the survey sample size increases accordingly—in a context similar to how individuals watch television (e.g., at home, alone). These surveys give us the ability to control or randomize the order in which respondents view the ads, to test candidates' ads in the context of the opposition ads, and to try out different creative treatments against control samples. Testing ads online can also be done relatively quickly—in a matter of days—whereas focus groups can take up to two weeks to recruit respondents.

Web surveys can be used to test other kinds of campaign communication as well. For example, with the rise of e-mail and other forms of virtual communication, it has gotten more difficult to reach voters using direct mail—there is a high burden on mail to break through when the majority of mail people receive is junk. Employing a "mailbox exercise," Web surveys can be used to test different creative treatments; with this experiment, separate samples of respondents see a Web page with different kinds of mail pieces such as a Crate and Barrel catalog, a credit card application, a fund-raising appeal, and a piece of political direct mail. We ask them to pick out the piece of mail they would be most likely to read. By varying the piece of political mail, we can get a sense of what would be most likely to be read by recipients when campaign mail reaches their door. We found in one experiment, for example, a direct mail piece with a voter registration form that looks like a quasi-government document is more effective than a mail piece that tells people why it is important to register to vote.

Of course, these studies are subject to the same concerns about representativeness, though the experimental work has internal validity as long as respondents are randomly assigned to treatment groups. But it is our experience that these results often hold up in the real world. We have validated the results of ad testing in Web panels with media market tests in which we place media buys in test and control markets, run the ads we tested online, and gauge their effectiveness with pre- and posttracking surveys. We found that the ads that tested well online tended to "work" better in the real world of politics, too.

Micro-Targeting

Since the early part of this decade, political operatives have been increasingly interested in more sophisticated ways of targeting voters. Surveys can provide campaigns with strategic targeting advice such as reaching out to groups like "soccer moms," "security moms," or more mundane, independent voters or college-educated men. In practice, however, refined segmentation of the electorate is rarely actionable because the voter files used for voter contact do not contain information like voters' attitudes on education or terrorism or even basic demographics like education level or income. Rather, they primarily contain very basic information like age, gender, and sometimes race. So campaigns rely on polling to determine whom they are trying to reach in their television buys or direct mail plans, but rarely can they use the detailed targeting advice from their pollsters beyond some basic demographic and geographic categories.

The most important innovation in this area came from Republicans following the 2000 presidential election, when they began to adopt techniques used in commercial research geared at more efficiently targeting potential customers.[5] Specifically, these operatives believed that political research needed to move beyond demographics and geography to focus on lifestyle as a way of understanding how people make political decisions. In their view, lifestyle choices such as which beer a person drinks could be predictive of political behavior, so that a Budweiser drinker might vote Republican while a foreign-import drinker might vote Democratic.

The key to harnessing this information for politics lies in the massive consumer databases owned by companies such as Claritas, InfoUSA, and Acxiom. These companies collect financial information about nearly everyone in America who has some sort of credit history, as well as data related to consumer choices such as car ownership, hobbies, and pet ownership. Republican operatives married these consumer data with polling data, as well as the information contained in voter files like vote history and party registration, to produce models predictive of being a Republican supporter or swing voter. They used these lists to build the fabled seventy-two-hour plan, which allowed them to target and mobilize voters successfully in 2002 and 2004.

The key to making micro-targeting work is that the drivers of these models come not from survey data but from the voter files and consumer data. In other words, the data (i.e., independent variables) that inform the models must exist on many or most of the voter records so that the results of the model can be applied back to individual voters. These models allow us to score individual voters' information such as their propensity to vote Democratic or Republican or their probability of taking a certain position on issues such as abortion or gay marriage. Political and advocacy campaigns can draw lists of base and persuadable voters from these data and contact them directly through the mail, over the phone, and at the door. Equally as important, this contact can include customized messaging that has much more precision than advertising over the airwaves. Certain types of base supporters or persuadable voters can receive messages tailored specifically to their concerns.

Micro-targeting does rely, at least in part, on interviewing respondents. It is possible that we are seeing the beginning of analysis of public opinion data that does not rely on interviewing individual voters. There are a range of data sources that provide valuable information about not just what people think about issues but emerging trends as well. Google offers tools on its site that allow the user to analyze word searches over time. These analyses could be as basic as seeing whose name is being searched more frequently in the presidential election (e.g., "Obama" or "McCain") or the words people are using to do research on health care reform (e.g., socialism). It is also possible to think about systematic analysis of political blogs, comments on articles, or content on social networking sites.

Experimentation

Political polling has some profound limitations when it comes to measuring the impact of direct voter contact. Tracking polling gauges aggregate shifts in opinion in reaction to news events or advertising, allowing campaigns to make adjustments to campaign strategy. But the impact of individual ads, direct mail pieces, phone calls, or door knocks is much harder to measure. Political pollsters have been influenced by the work of Don Green and Alan Gerber, who use controlled experiments to measure how different forms of voter contact affect voter registration and turnout.[6] They find, for instance, that in-person contact and direct mail are much more effective than telephone calls in actually getting voters to the polls. Their research explores not just the modes of contact but also the substantive content of contact. They find that content of the messaging is not really that important, but simply receiving contact matters a great deal. In their work, generic outreach that emphasizes civic duty was as effective as—if not more effective than—outreach that included a substantive message on why it was important to vote.

Pollsters are beginning to incorporate experimentation into their own research for campaigns. The experiments in Web-based research noted above are becoming quite common, but real-world experiments are emerging as well. Pollsters, working with mail, phone, and list vendors, are participating in controlled experiments in which they attempt to measure the impact of individual mail pieces and phone calls and the combination of mail and phone contact. The actual effectiveness can be measured with pre- and postsurveys of recipients of mail and phone calls, against control groups, to see whether attitudes move in response to treatment. If the goal is voter mobilization, the impact of mail and phone can be measured by examining voter files to determine whether treatment groups turned out at higher rates than control groups.

The stereotypes about political polling suggest that craven politicians use polling to regularly measure their standing with voters and adjust positions with the shifting winds. The reality is that few politicians below the level of the president have the resources to conduct regular polls, let alone reinvent themselves in an ongoing manner. Instead, political polling is most useful to candidates when it provides strategic information on how to best communicate themselves and their policies and to shape their interaction with voters. Traditional landline political polling continues to do yeoman's work in providing precisely that kind of information to campaigns but is also confronting real limitations wrought by changes in communications technology and the rise of new media. Moreover, this methodology is inherently limiting, as it measures opinion from the top down and cannot easily incorporate views formed from the bottom up.

At the same time, the profession is well equipped with a range of creative alternatives that overcome some of these changes and even expand the way we think of the very definition of public opinion. Of course, the political world is not interested in these approaches merely as an academic exercise; the research needs to be affordable and accurate and produce actionable, strategic advice. Political polling is not there yet, but it is well on its way.

NOTES

1. Accuracy is a critical issue for campaign pollsters. Unlike with surveys conducted for media outlets, there are real consequences for getting the "horse race" wrong; horse race numbers impact strategic decision making like resource allocation or the campaigns' thematic approach (e.g., attack or not attack your opponent). Moreover, developing a reputation for inaccurate measurement can have a negative impact on landing business.

2. Susan Herbst, *Numbered Voices: How Opinion Polling Has Shaped American Politics* (Chicago: University of Chicago Press, 1993).

3. Knowledge Networks, which recruits its panel through RDD sampling, maintains a representative Internet panel.

4. At a minimum, Web-based surveys have the benefits of self-administered surveys, particularly with regard to sensitive questions. In other words, we can ask sensitive questions without concern about the impact of the interviewer or even eliminate interviewer bias altogether.

5. Douglas B. Sosnik, Matthew J. Dowd, and Ron Fournier, *Applebee's America* (New York: Simon and Schuster, 2006).

6. Donald P. Green and Alan S. Gerber, *Get Out The Vote: How to Increase Voter Turnout,* 2nd ed. (Washington, DC: Brookings Institution Press, 2008).

8

Transitioning into a New Era of Public Opinion Research

KIRBY GOIDEL

When we first began this book project, we considered several different titles: *Public Opinion at the Gallows* or *Dewey Wins! Polling's Next Great Catastrophe*. We decided these titles were too alarmist. There can be little question that public opinion research is going through its most significant transition since telephone interviews replaced face-to-face interviews as the primary data collection mode during the 1970s, but there is also little question that opinion polling will adapt and survive. No other technique or methodology so eloquently and efficiently captures the democratic voice. And no other social science methodology has proven to be as useful to political elites and journalists for understanding, mobilizing, or moving public support.

The Economic Demand for Public Opinion Polling

In an information age, public opinion polling continues to be a good economic value, providing politicos with strategic and actionable information. For candidates, political parties, and interest groups, polling helps to reduce the uncertainty inherent in campaigning and the policy-making process. With poll results, messages can be more effectively framed and targeted to specific audiences, while the effect of these messages can be monitored and tracked. Campaigns use this information to alter strategy, frame and reframe messages, or alter the targets of communications. For the news media, polling helps to write the campaign narrative, providing an overarching theme for framing individual news stories. Campaign events, for example, are often interpreted in light of falling or rising poll numbers: the struggling campaign desperately trying to right itself or the successful campaign pressing its advantage.

The pervasiveness of polling in American politics may boil down to a simple economic proposition. Public opinion polls will continue to play an important role in American politics as long as the perceived value of the data is greater than the costs of conducting the poll and analyzing the results. Growing cell-phone-only and cell-phone-mostly populations, for example, appear to have had little or no effect on the demand for polling data. Indeed, even as pollsters caution about potential coverage and nonresponse biases, the number of polls and the number of polling firms appear to have increased. Perhaps this is to be expected. If we think of polling as part of an effort by campaigns and candidates to reduce uncertainty, less certainty in any given set of results may increase the need for more polling. Despite concerns that a "perfect storm" was brewing during the 2008 presidential election,[1] it may well have been the most polled election in our history. And more people will be asked more times by more polling organizations if they approve or disapprove of President Barack Obama than was the case with regard to any other president in our history.

There is little reason to suspect the amount of polling activity will subside in the near future. The form of polling, however, will undoubtedly change, as will our understanding of what makes for a "good" poll. The landline telephone survey based on random digit dialing (RDD), and the mainstay of survey research since the 1970s, will move first to an endangered species list and eventually toward extinction. It is not clear what exactly will replace it—online surveys, cell phone surveys, and addressed-based sampling are likely candidates—but there is little question that changes in technology and communication patterns are moving us away from the household phone and toward cell phones and other mobile personal communication devices. Survey research will follow. The need to understand public preferences on everything from candidate choice to consumer behavior for strategic political and rational economic actors is simply too great to be left to chance. If the past is prologue, marketing and political professionals will lead the way as they struggle to find cost-effective mechanisms for providing clients with actionable data.

For critics of online surveys and other "new" survey methodologies, it is important to remember that roughly four decades ago researchers questioned the accuracy of telephone interviews, with some methods texts warning readers away from using telephone interviews altogether.[2] In his Presidential Address to the American Association of Public Opinion Research in 2002, Don Dillman recalled being routinely dismissed for having not learned the lessons of the *Literary Digest* poll when he began conducting telephone interviews in the 1970s. Less than a decade later, Dillman observed, "the telephone had moved from being an unrecognized possibility to an accepted method of data collection."[3] There is an obvious parallel to today, but the challenges are even more striking. We are fast reaching the day when, thanks to nonresponse and an ever growing cell-only population, traditional telephone surveys will no longer be representative of public opinion. At the same time, we have greater access than ever before to opinion voluntarily expressed and easily captured in various online forums. Such opinion may not be randomly drawn or representative, but it may provide a richer understanding of public opinion than can be captured in a standardized survey questionnaire.

There is also little question that technological change has altered the nature of public opinion. When Susan Herbst wrote *Numbered Voices,* she noted that public opinion and the public opinion poll had become interchangeable. Public opinion was the statistical aggregation of privately held beliefs as measured by polls and reported in the news media.[4] Within this paradigm, polls could easily reveal that 52 percent of Americans approved of the president or 42 percent opposed health care reform. Public opinion continues to be expressed in this manner, particularly presidential approval ratings and trial heat questions in election surveys. But our thinking about public opinion—even when quantified—has changed in important ways. Analysts are much more likely to think about segments of the public, cross-pressured and persuadable, soccer moms and NASCAR dads. And though public opinion scholars have long cautioned that term "public opinion" is a misnomer and that we should think instead about multiple publics, it has been only recently that these multiple publics have become the defining characteristic of public opinion. In a digital age, public opinion is less about statistical aggregation and more about segmentation.

Because individuals are now subject to a wider range of information flows, public opinion is also more elusive, particularly when we move beyond candidate polling and into the "fuzzy" arena of issue polling.[5] This is a point also made by Susan Herbst; polls of candidate preference are valid and often revealing because the choice is fixed and ultimately validated with election returns. But what can opinion polls tell us about more nebulous issues, such as health care reform or support of the Iraq War or additional troops in Afghanistan, for which we lack a suitable baseline to check reported responses against some measure of reality? These are not new concerns: scholars have long contended that issue preferences are unstable and vary according to context and question wording. But these concerns take on a renewed import when information flows are more varied and when the public is more segmented into increasingly distinct audiences. Public opinion in this context is more elusive to measure and less meaningful when aggregated.

To illustrate the point, consider the following survey question asked by Louis Harris and Associates in April 1974:

It has been proposed that Congress pass a comprehensive health insurance program which would combine federal government, employer, and employee contributions into one federal health insurance system that would cover all medical and health expenses. Opponents say that would get the federal government too much into medicine and health care. Supporters say such insurance is necessary for people to obtain proper coverage. Do you favor or oppose such a comprehensive federal health insurance program?

Fifty-four percent of respondents in the 1974 survey favored a comprehensive health insurance policy, 28 percent opposed, and 18 percent were unsure. Now imagine that the same question was asked today with identical results—would the interpretation be the same? In contemporary politics, the public conversation is more varied, the information flow is considerably more diverse (at least in the aggregate), and public opinion is more difficult to interpret as a statistical aggregate.

If we care about our ability to draw representative samples that provide reasonably accurate estimates of population parameters (and we should), we need new methodological tools. But we also need to give additional thought to what we are measuring, what it means, and how well it can be represented by aggregated responses to fixed-choice survey questions.

One of the primary challenges in redefining survey methodology involves balancing data quality against survey costs—and ensuring that quality is not the loser in this equation. It has always been the case that researchers have balanced costs against quality. The most common realization is in decisions about sampling size and margin of error. The movement to telephone interviews and RDD sampling during the 1970s was also driven by evidence that the data collected through telephone interviews were accurate enough particularly given significant reductions in data collection costs. Perhaps the greatest challenge is ensuring that the lower costs of online surveys and news organization straw polls do not undermine more accurate and expensive data collection methods relying on randomly drawn samples. Mark Blumenthal's call for a rating system based on transparency in methodology and a more active role for professional organizations such as the American Association of Public Opinion Research (AAPOR) and Council for Marketing and Opinion Research (CMOR) is an important part of this. The equilibrium between costs and quality, however, will likely be determined through market forces. How much accuracy are clients willing to pay for? These pressures are much more significant for professional pollsters who may not be able to work costly cell phone samples into their data collection efforts. Even without the addition of cell phone samples, traditional polling is growing more expensive as response rates continue to decline and respondents grow more skeptical of unsolicited telephone calls. So how much accuracy is good enough relative to a given set of costs?

In a professional sense, polls provide important information regarding two questions: (1) How well can we estimate a population parameter based on our sampling techniques (e.g., vote choice or market share)? and (2) How well can we identify what moves public preferences from one candidate, one side of an issue, or one product to another? To achieve the first objective, random samples are a necessary ingredient. To achieve the second, nonrandom samples may be sufficient, particularly to the extent that they can incorporate the elements of experimental design or target very specific or hard-to-reach populations. Anna Greenberg, for example, notes that her firm's research indicates that online tests of advertisements are as effective as market tests relying on pretest and posttest surveys. Experimental work on what mobilizes voter turnout has similarly been instructive for campaign get-out-the-vote efforts. As polls grow more expensive and potentially less accurate, other ways of understanding public opinion become more enticing.

This brings us to one of the more important points of this particular volume made separately and in different ways by each of the respective authors. While there is good reason for concern about the accuracy of public opinion polls in light of growing nonresponse and cell-only populations, there is far greater reason for optimism. The innovative work going on at the Pew Center is illustrative of the type of research being done to better understand the shortcomings of traditional polling and the potential of newer methodologies (e.g., dual-frame sampling) or, in some cases, a return to older methodologies (e.g., address-based sampling) to best reflect public preferences. There is more than just methodological tweaking afoot. Our understanding of what constitutes "good" polling, Mark Blumenthal observes, has changed dramatically in recent years. Polling practices that once would have been considered taboo (e.g., IVR polling) have proven to be reasonably accurate predictors of election outcomes, while traditional indicators of performance (e.g., response rates) have proven to be less important than was once thought. More broadly, there is a tremendous amount of work being devoted to understanding how to best measure public opinion and a parallel line of research on the democratic implications of online opinion expression. As a result, we may have better understanding of public opinion—and better tools to measure public opinion—in five to ten years than at any time in our history.

The question remains as to whether public opinion scholars and pollsters can better capture public opinion as conversation (as opposed to counting). As Susan Herbst observes, that conversation—ongoing, dynamic, and interactive—is more accessible than ever before. The development of digital media has provided an expanding array of opportunities for citizens to engage in political talk. The willingness of citizens to take advantage of these opportunities to express their opinions in online forums or blogs or by commenting on news stories or reports is quite remarkable. Arguably, online opinion expression is dominated by the most intensely partisan and ideological citizens, and, more often than not, these citizens are talking to like-minded friends, family, and acquaintances. Nevertheless, these conversations are increasingly public, captured through online media, and subject to investigation. They provide the opportunity to place numeric representations of public opinion (public opinion as counting) within the deeper and richer context of political conversation.

It should come as little surprise that professional pollsters are making use of these technologies in a variety of innovative ways. This includes online testing of advertising, online focus groups, experiments, and interviews that allow respondents to provide greater depth to their responses and reveal meaning that might be missing from quantitative counts. Online focus groups, Anna Greenberg notes, provided early warning signs about Sarah Palin in 2008 even as her poll numbers remained quite strong.

The big picture is this: while we have more reasons to be concerned about the accuracy of opinion polls, we also have a tremendous opportunity to better understand public opinion as fluid, dynamic, and interactive. Pollsters will continue to count preferences as long as there is a market demand or interest in what their fellow citizens think, do, and believe, but they may also be better positioned to capture the conversation that drives politics. In doing so, they may bring us further away from a definition of public opinion as statistical aggregate and closer to understanding it as defined by V. O. Key Jr.: "as those opinions held by private persons which governments find it useful to heed."[6]

Journalists, Citizens, Bloggers, and Polling Literacy

Perhaps, as critics note, polling matters too much. Horse race coverage during a campaign overwhelms issues, while issue-based polling too often distorts—rather than reflects—public preferences. Respondents are asked not to think or consider but to react. These criticisms ring true even among many pollsters who note that too often nonattitudes pass for meaningful public opinion. Polls on health care reform, for example, may be given undue importance even as pollsters (and others) warn that the public is woefully uninformed about specific proposals or the details of health care legislation. Missing is an understanding of the range of what the public might (or might not) support or what public opinion might look like if it were more (or fully) informed. David Moore has perhaps made this point as well as anyone in noting the range of public support on the Iraq War. According to Moore, opinion on the war was much more permissive—and less directive—than common interpretations of poll results suggested. The difference is important because, although Americans supported going to war as a policy alternative, they were hardly demanding the invasion of Iraq.[7] Even so, public opinion was treated as though it were a fixed commodity and was subsequently used in the policy debate as a mechanism for muting public criticism of the war effort. A broader critique can be found among proponents of deliberative polling and in efforts to model fully informed public opinion. On many of the most pressing policy issues, the public often lacks stable, well-defined preferences.

Herein lies the rub: despite the growing challenge of cell-only and cell-mostly populations, despite growing concerns of coverage and nonresponse bias, the primary challenge confronting pollsters is not technical. The numbers are what they are—a limited snapshot of public opinion at a given moment in time contingent upon specific question wordings, interviewing techniques, sampling methods, and the construction of sample weights and likely voters. Most pollsters well understand the limitations of their data and—at least privately—acknowledge these limitations. No, the primary challenge confronting polling resides in providing meaningful interpretations of the numbers: the careful analysis, the deeper understanding of context, and the comparison of one set of poll results with the range of existing results. As Susan Herbst might contend, it is the gap between a specific methodology (polling) and a nebulous concept (public opinion) that the method only imperfectly captures and reflects.

At this point, it might be easy to resort to clichés about the need for greater polling literacy. Polling, like so much of American politics, is not something that is well understood by the average citizen. With misunderstanding comes distrust. The public can hardly be blamed for its skepticism. Survey results vary from day to day and from question to question. This gives the impression that pollsters can generate any set of findings they want or that one poll is just as good as any other poll. This point goes beyond survey research. Citizens and journalists have—at best—vague understandings of the differences between chance and systematic variation. For this reason, polling literacy can only take us so far. A public that has trouble remembering the names of its elective representatives is unlikely to understand the details of random sampling, questionnaire design, nonresponse error, or coverage bias.

The problem is made worse by news reports that trumpet outliers—the one poll among dozens that shows a tightening race or that challenges conventional understanding of public opinion on a leading issue. Polls that make the best news may not reflect the best polling or our best understanding of public opinion at a given moment in time. One might imagine vigilant journalists sifting through the poll results to decipher good from bad, but the traditional news media are increasingly ill suited to evaluating the meaning of public opinion aside from a specific finding. The problem may be worse than simply misinterpreting the findings from individual polls. In a postmortem on news coverage of the 2004 presidential election, Tom Rosenstiel observed that newsroom cutbacks and twenty-four-hour news cycles have expanded the use of polls as news, made coverage of the campaign more horse race–oriented and superficial, and led to the use of less credible polling in news broadcasts.[8] Johanna Dunaway similarly reports that as the resources devoted to political reporting decline, the amount of horse race coverage increases. Horse race coverage becomes an easy substitute for more substantive and meaningful coverage.

The increasing polarization of news audiences and programming since 2004 has undoubtedly contributed further to declining confidence in polling as talking heads cite different poll results to score political points and as pollsters use new media outlets to bypass traditional news outlets. As a practical matter, there is less of a filter on what polling enters the public conversation and less critical analysis of what the results mean. The quote from Tom Jensen, the director of Public Policy Polling, in Mark Blumenthal's chapter is particularly instructive. Able to release results directly through his organization's blog, he no longer feels reliant on traditional media (in this case the *Washington Post*) to disseminate results.

The politicization of polling should concern pollsters for another reason. One can reasonably argue that the advent of telephone polling in the 1970s and particularly the widespread adoption of in-house polling organizations by news outlets allowed for a deeper understanding of social change and provided journalists with a basis for challenging elite interpretations of events.[9] Increasingly, however, news organizations are cutting their in-house polling operations, while polls are used selectively to spin events or political issues. Not only do many news outlets lack the capacity to conduct independent polling, but they also lack the expertise to provide a critical interpretation of what any given poll means. There is an unhealthy synergy at play: lacking an understanding of polling, citizens need news organizations to serve as gatekeepers, sifting through poll results to develop and communicate an informed understanding of public opinion. Unfortunately, news organizations increasingly lack the resources to perform this gatekeeping function. The result has been more polls covered with less depth and understanding. But even when news organizations decide not to cover a poll, online media provide a readily available source for disseminating results.

The good news is that if online media provide aspiring pollsters with the opportunity to bypass traditional news organizations and disseminate their findings directly to a wider audience, they also open the door to public comment and criticism. The most widely noted case involves Nate Silver's analysis of Strategic Vision, Inc., a Republican polling firm that has been censured by the American Association of Public Opinion Research for failing to disclose information about its methodology. After conducting a statistical analysis of the data, Silver found something afoul in the pattern of numbers released by Strategic Vision, a peculiar and highly unlikely set of results that, for Silver, suggested the strong possibility of fraud. More recently, Markos Moulitsas of Daily Kos sued his former pollster R2000 after a similar analysis indicated the data were likely fabricated. As Moulitsas concluded, "The weekly Research 2000 State of the Nation poll we ran the past year and a half was likely bunk."[10]

The episode raised a larger question addressed by Mark Blumenthal in his *National Journal* column: How do we know if a pollster is simply "making up the numbers"? Blumenthal's answer is that we can't:

In an old media world, we received polling data from a few trusted media brands. If CBS News and the *New York Times* said they did a poll, then we trusted that they did a poll. But in the new media world, we are confronted with polls from sources we have barely heard of, including some organizations that appear to exist solely for the purpose of disseminating polls.[11]

So how do we know if we can trust a given poll? For Blumenthal, the solution resides in increased transparency. Perhaps we cannot be certain if an organization is making up the results, but we can require minimal standards for transparency so that the methods can be known and evaluated.

His suggestion for a rating system for the level of disclosure would be useful on several levels. First, if constructed as an easy heuristic, say along the lines of PolitiFact's Truth-O-Meter, it could help guide citizen and journalist understanding of poll results. Second, to the extent that the disclosure rating is taken seriously by the more established pollsters, it could also create an incentive for greater disclosure. The challenge—also noted by Blumenthal—is convincing pollsters that this an industry problem that must be confronted. The reality is that citizens lack the understanding or interest to critically evaluate polls, while journalists lack the resources to provide the sort of depth and context necessary for meaningful analyses of public opinion. Twenty-four-hour news cycles and online media mean, as well, that questionable polling practices will continue to make it into the public conversation about campaigns, politics, and policy. A guide as to which polls can be trusted—and which should be viewed with skepticism—would be tremendously valuable.

Unfortunately, transparency can only take us so far if the meaning of public opinion—and not its measurement—is our greatest concern. Sites like Pollster.com also provide careful and nuanced interpretations of poll results, including comparisons with the range of reported results on a given question. Thus journalists and citizens have at their fingertips sophisticated analyses of public opinion data. The challenge is in ensuring that these more careful analyses are not replaced by superficial news coverage or, worse, coverage that distorts public opinion by highlighting statistical outliers.

Matthew Nisbet, a communication scholar at American University, has done extensive work on science communication. One of his conclusions is that scientists must be more active in the public conversation over the meaning of their work.[12] Otherwise news coverage of science achieves a false balance on "science controversies" such as embryonic stem cell research, global warming, and the teaching of evolution. Pollsters and public opinion scholars would do well to heed his advice and to ensure that they are—as a community of scholars and professional practitioners—actively engaged in the public meaning of public opinion. This means not only commenting on poll results but also the creation and support of Web sites and blogs to provide public comment on findings and methodology. If online media can be used to disseminate results and bypass the traditional media, it can also be used as an important check on the methodology and meaning of public opinion.

Polling continues to play an important role in American politics, not only in providing strategic information but in giving voice to citizens who may not attend town halls, write blog posts, or comment on news stories. The great history of public opinion polling is that, despite its shortcomings, it has been and can continue to be a democratic force, challenging elite interpretations of events and moderating the most vocal and intensely partisan citizens. Polling can continue to play this role, but only to the extent that it is trusted as a valid and reliable indicator of public preferences. This means disclosure, but it also means renewed attention to how polls are being used in the news and the blogosphere and a more active engagement in the meaning of public opinion. The meaning and measurement of public opinion will undoubtedly change, but the commitment to giving voice to the citizenry—and fairly reflecting public preferences—should not.

NOTES

1. Mark Blumenthal, "Pollsters Facing Elections Perfect Storm," *National Journal,* October 8, 2008, www.msnbc.msn.com/id/27084438/ (accessed May 14, 2009).

2. Charles Backstrom and Gerald Hursch, *Survey Research* (Evanston, IL: Northwestern University Press, 1963).

3. Don Dillman, "Presidential Address: Navigating the Rapids of Change: Some Observations on Survey Methodology in the Early Twenty-First Century," *Public Opinion Quarterly* 66 (2002): 473–94, 475.

4. Susan Herbst, *Numbered Voices: How Opinion Polling Has Shaped American Politics* (Chicago: University of Chicago Press, 1993).

5. Cliff Young, "Young and Amic: Polling on Fuzzy Issues Like Healthcare Reform—You Can't Measure What Doesn't Exist," Pollster.com, November 30, 2009, www.pollster.com/blogs/

young_and_amic_polling_on_fuzzy_issues_like_healthcare_reform_you_cant_measure_what_doesnt_exist.php (accessed April 9, 2010).

6. V. O. Key Jr., *Public Opinion and American Democracy* (New York: Knopf, 1961).

7. David Moore, *The Opinion Makers: An Insider Exposes the Truth behind the Polls* (Boston: Beacon Press, 2008).

8. Tom Rosenstiel, "Political Polling and the New Media Culture: The Case of More Being Less," *Public Opinion Quarterly* 65 (2005): 698–716.

9. Andrew Kohut, "Polls," in *The Politics of News, the News of Politics*, ed. Doris Graber, Denis McQuail, and Pippa Norris, 150–70 (Washington, DC: CQ Press, 2007).

10. Nate Silver, "Strategic Vision Polls Exhibit Unusual Patterns, Possibly Indicating Fraud," www.fivethirtyeight.com/2009/09/strategic-vision-polls-exhibit-unusual.html (accessed July 17, 2010); Daily Kos, "More on Research 2000," June 29, 2010, www.dailykos.com/story/2010/6/29/880185/-More-on-Research-2000 (accessed July 22, 2010).

11. Mark Blumenthal, "Strategic Vision and the Transparency Gap," *National Journal,* September 28, 2009, www.nationaljournal.com/njonline/mp_20090925_5674.php (accessed April 9, 2010).

12. Matthew Nisbet and Chris Mooney, "Thanks for the Facts, Now Sell Them," *Washington Post,* April 15, 2007, www.washingtonpost.com/wp-dyn/content/article/2007/04/13/AR2007041302064.html (accessed April 9, 2010).

CONTRIBUTORS

MARK BLUMENTHAL is editor and publisher of Pollster.com, the Web site that publishes poll results and a daily running commentary that explains, demystifies, and critiques political polling for political insiders and the general public. Pollster.com is partly an outgrowth of Blumenthal's Mystery Pollster blog, which he started in September 2004. As a polling analyst for the *National Journal,* Blumenthal writes a weekly column for NationalJournal.com. In May 2007, along with Pollster.com co-creator Charles Franklin, Blumenthal received the Warren J. Mitofsky Innovators Award from the American Association for Public Opinion Research (AAPOR). In 2005, the National Council on Public Polls awarded Blumenthal and the Mystery Pollster blog a special citation for its work explaining polls to the Internet reader. Blumenthal has been in the political polling business for more than twenty years, conducting and analyzing political polls and focus groups for Democratic candidates and market research surveys for major corporations. In January 2007, after fifteen years with his former partners David Petts and Anna Bennett in the firm Bennett, Petts and Blumenthal (BPB), he decided to devote all of his time to Pollster.com. He earned a political science degree from the University of Michigan and has done course work toward a master's degree in the Joint Program in Survey Methodology (JPSM) at the University of Maryland. He has guest-lectured at American University and at training seminars sponsored by EMILY's List, the Democratic National Committee, and the National Democratic Institute for International Affairs. He served as communications chair of the American Association for Public Opinion Research from 2007 to 2008.

CHARLIE COOK is publisher of *The Cook Political Report* and political analyst for the National Journal Group, writing weekly for *National Journal* magazine and *CongressDailyAM*. Widely regarded as one of the nation's leading authorities on U.S. elections and political trends, Charlie has appeared on the ABC, CBS, and NBC evening news programs, *Meet the Press,* and *This Week.* He has served as an election night analyst for NBC since 1994. The *New York Times* has called Cook "one of the best political handicappers in the nation" and noted that *The Cook Political Report* is "a newsletter that both parties regard as authoritative."

JOHANNA DUNAWAY received her master's and Ph.D. degrees from Rice University. Her interests include mass media, politics, and public opinion. She teaches media and policy processes and introduction to political communication at Louisiana State University. Dr. Dunaway was previously an assistant professor in the Department of Political Science at Sam Houston State University. Specifically, her research focuses on the news media as an institution, influences on political news content, and the impact of media messages on political attitudes and behavior. She has published research in the *Journal of Politics, Political Research Quarterly, Policy Studies Journal,* and *Social Science Quarterly.*

ROBERT "KIRBY" GOIDEL is director of Louisiana State University's Manship School Research Facility, which includes the Public Policy Research Lab and the Media Effects Lab. As senior public policy fellow of the Reilly Center for Media & Public Affairs, he directs the annual Louisiana Survey and provides analysis of the findings to government agencies, nonprofit organizations, and the media. Goidel works closely with diverse constituencies to develop survey instruments, analyze data, prepare reports,and present research findings. His received his Ph.D. in political science from the University of Kentucky and is the author of two books and numerous journal articles. He is a professor in the Manship School of Mass Communication and the Dpartment of Political Science.

ANNA GREENBERG is a leading Democratic pollster and polling expert. She advises campaigns, advocacy organizations, and foundations in the

United States and has helped elect Congressman Rahm Emanuel (IL-5), Congresswoman Gabrielle Giffords (AZ-8), and Senator Amy Klobuchar (MN). She has worked closely with a wide range of groups including the AFL-CIO, EMILY's List, Women's Voices. Women Vote (WVWV), USAction, and MoveOn.org. Greenberg is one of America's leading experts in public opinion and religion, youth, and women's health and conducts research on religion and values in public life for *Religion and Ethics Newsweekly* and the United Nations Foundation and on women's health for the National Women's Health Resource Center, the American Psychological Association, and the Association of Reproductive Health Professionals. Through her firm, Greenberg Quinlan Rosner, she directs work with the W. K. Kellogg Foundation and the Center for Rural Strategies and has helped shape and advance the center's research program on perceptions of rural America. Greenberg is a leading expert in research with difficult-to-reach audiences, Web-based research, and ad testing and directs Greenberg Quinlan Rosner's innovations in advanced micro-targeting and segmentation analysis. Greenberg has taught at Harvard University's John F. Kennedy School of Government and was a visiting scholar with the Pew Research Center for the People & the Press. She serves on the advisory board of the Center for Reproductive Rights and the Boisi Center for Religion and American Public Life at Boston College and is a research fellow at American University's Center for Congressional and Presidential Studies. She holds a B.A. in government from Cornell University and a Ph.D. in political science from the University of Chicago.

DR. SUSAN HERBST is executive vice chancellor for the University System of Georgia and professor of public policy. Her research focuses on public opinion, mass media, and the nature of the policy-making process in the United States. Previously, she was professor and chair of the Department of Political Science at Northwestern University, dean of liberal arts at Temple University, and provost at the University of Albany/SUNY, where she also served as acting president from 2006 to 2007. She is the editor of a book series on American politics, public opinion, and political behavior published by the University of Chicago Press. Her current work focuses on the nature of public opinion in the United States and, most recently, the ways that media shape presidential political speeches and rhetoric. Dr. Herbst earned her bachelor's degree with honors in political science from Duke University, Durham, North Carolina, and a doctorate in communication theory and research from the University of Southern California, Annenberg School for Communications, Los Angeles.

SCOTT KEETER is director of survey research for the Pew Research Center in Washington, D.C. His published work includes books on political participation and civic engagement, religion and politics, public opinion, and American elections, along with articles and chapters on survey methodology, political communications, and health care topics. A native of North Carolina, he attended Davidson College as an undergraduate and received a Ph.D. in political science from the University of North Carolina at Chapel Hill. He has taught at George Mason University, Rutgers University, and Virginia Commonwealth University. Since 1980, Keeter has been an election night analyst of exit polls for NBC News and has served as standards chair and councilor-at-large for the American Association for Public Opinion Research.

ASHLEY KIRZINGER is a doctoral student at the Manship School of Mass Communication. She earned her M.A. in communication studies at Wake Forest University, where she taught public speaking and studied religious rhetoric in political campaigns. Her current research interests include public opinion, deliberative democracy, and media effects on political attitudes. She is originally from Louisville, Kentucky, and received her B.A. from Denison University in Granville, Ohio.

MICHAEL XENOS earned his Ph.D. from the University of Washington in 2005. His interests include political communication and public opinion. He teaches new media and other communications courses. From 2005 to 2008 he served as an assistant professor at the University of Wisconsin, where he was awarded summer research grants in 2006 and 2007.

INDEX